COMMENTS O
# Kenneth C. Ulmer

Ken Ulmer is one of America's new voices, rising with a penetrating call to pragmatic spiritual dynamics. As a Christian leader, he stands tall; as a servant to society, he stands out; as a friend, he stands trustworthy; as a man of God, he stands close—in touch with our Father, that he might be in touch with Him whose touch can change the world. Knowing Dr. Ulmer as I do, I attest to this: the man is real to the core! The truths with which he inspires multitudes becomes real and livable because he is relating what he's learned and lived and proven.

**Jack W. Hayford**
President, The King's University
Founding Pastor, The Church On The Way, Van Nuys, California

Dr. Ulmer is one of the most strategic Christian leaders in the nation. His impact in helping people understand God's principles for life is enriching while remaining biblical. It is hard to overstate the impact Dr. Ulmer makes on tens of thousands of Christians every week.

**Dr. Mark Brewer**
President, All Saints College, Denver, Colorado

Dr. Ken Ulmer does what he does best. He slices through the confusion, misunderstanding and misinformation and then clearly and accurately explains the Scripture.

**Robert Morris**
Bestselling Author, *The Blessed Life*

## *Making Your Money Count*

Pick up this book and prepare to be changed! . . .Clearly articulates biblically sound truth on the topic of money. . . . Ulmer brings us back to what the Bible really has to say on money and how we should use what we have.

**John Bevere**
Author and Speaker; Co-founder, Messenger International
Colorado Springs/Australia/United Kingdom

I would urge anyone who wants to know God's process for lifting peo-ple from poverty to financial productivity and wise money manage-ment to read this book! If you deal with money—whether you are rich, poor or in between—this book is for you. If you want to learn how to ease your monetary struggles . . . and help others who may be strug-gling financially, this book shows you how. It contains new thinking on a psychological and biblical foundation that I applaud.

**Dr. Robert H. Schuller**
Founding Pastor, Crystal Cathedral, Garden Grove, California

A benchmark book by a dynamic scholar preacher that is inspiring and instructive. . . . In this powerful and penetrating book, Bishop Ulmer plumbs the depths of the biblical meaning of prosperity. He confronts the false teaching of both the divine right presumption and the anti-prosperity predispositions in contemporary Christianity. . . . Ulmer is one of the truly great spiritual leaders of our time.

**Dr. Lloyd Ogilvie**
Former Chaplin, U.S. Senate

It's a special delight to commend this evenhanded, insightful, and practical tool that untwists a subject that's too often mangled by poor exposition or distorted by exaggeration. . . . a solid resource from a leader who provides us with the whole package: a book written by a wise pastor, a balanced teacher, a thorough-going scholar, a Bible-preacher, and a passionate and godly man. Through *Making Your Money Count*, stewarding our finances is made alive and done right!

**Jack W. Hayford**
President, The King's University
Founding Pastor, The Church On The Way, Van Nuys, California

Among all the parables in the Bible, two-thirds speak to the issue of money. We all grapple with the question of how to be good stewards of our resources. What a blessing it is that Bishop Kenneth Ulmer has written a practical guide on the subject based on God's Word. Thank you, Bishop!

**Angela Bassett and Courtney B. Vance**
Actors

# The Champion in You

In a world that is filled with so many people who feel defeated or fearful this word comes at a needy time. Bishop Kenneth Ulmer shares insights that transforms the reader from the dismal to the dynamic. Take a read and watch the truths transform you until you emerge undaunted a champion for Christ!

**Bishop T.D. Jakes, Sr.**
Founder and Senior Pastor, The Potter's House of Dallas

My prayer is that as you read *The Champion in You* that God would stir in your heart that you would be a champion in your generation. We need men and women to stand up and champion the cause of God in our world. God has great things for you and you are a champion in Him!

**John Bevere**
Author and Speaker; Cofounder, Messenger International
Colorado Springs/Australia/United Kingdom

This book will unlock what God has destined each of us to be, and that is, a champion. This isn't some quick fix, gimmick-filled book. Bishop Ulmer gives practical biblical principles that will inform you and help you to lead a transformed and empowered life. This book will change your life.

**Bishop Noel Jones**
Senior Pastor, City of Refuge, Los Angeles, California

This is a very exciting book! It is a can't-put-it-down page-turner by one of today's most inspiring communicators. In *The Champion in You*, Kenneth Ulmer vividly portrays a divinely inspired, powerful biblical truth: God has placed within each of us a champion waiting to be discovered and released to be used for His glory and the encouragement of all those around us. If you want to get acquainted with this champion in you, this book will show you the way!

**Dr. Lloyd Ogilvie**
Former Chaplin, U.S. Senate

## The Power of Money: How to Avoid A Devil's Snare

Such a balanced Biblical teaching! This is a topic that too many preachers today teach as a "name it and claim it and blab it and grab it" theology. Bishop Ulmer has great wisdom and insight on the subject of mammon.

**Pastor Benny Hinn**
(As quoted on "This is Your Day")

## In His Image

My dear friend, Bishop Kenneth Ulmer, is one of the most outstanding, creative preachers of our time. With *In His Image*, he has given us creative biblical treasure that will not only capture our minds, but will also move our hearts toward a God whose heart is moved toward us. Reading this book will compel you to love God more deeply and to worship Him more fully!

**Dr. Crawford W. Loritts, Jr.**
Senior Pastor, Fellowship Bible Church, Roswell, Georgia

# PASSIONATE
# GOD

## Kenneth C. Ulmer

**Regal**

For more information and
special offers from Regal Books, email us at
subscribe@regalbooks.com

Published by Regal
From Gospel Light
Ventura, California, U.S.A.
*www.regalbooks.com*
Printed in the U.S.A.

Rights for publishing this book outside the U.S.A. or in non-English languages are
administered by Gospel Light Worldwide, an international not-for-profit ministry.
For additional information, please visit www.glww.org, email info@glww.org, or write to
Gospel Light Worldwide, 1957 Eastman Avenue, Ventura, CA 93003, U.S.A.

To order copies of this book and other Regal products in bulk quantities,
please contact us at 1-800-446-7735.

*To my five granddaughters,*
## *Kamryn, Ayari, Raegan, Aniya and Bailee:*

*I pray that you will come to know the God of your grandfather
and your mother and father. I pray this volume will one day teach
you to walk in the passionate love of the God of your salvation.
You are gifts from God.*

# Contents

# Contents

# Preface

How does God feel about you? Does He care about what you're going through? Is there a situation you face that He's ambivalent about? Does God even *have* feelings? We sing songs, hear poems, read Scriptures, hear sermons, listen to personal testimonies that imply that God is a caring God. Yet . . . sometimes, I wonder. Do you?

As I write these words, the minds and hearts of Americans have been stunned and captured by the tragedy that seized headlines around the world from the community of Newtown, Connecticut. Christmas 2012 will be forever etched in both the consciences and memories of a generation as another senseless, heartless demonstration of the inhumanity of man becomes another flashpoint in the debate on gun laws and another occasion to ask questions like, "Where was God when this happened?" or, "How could God allow this—doesn't He care?" or, "How can a good God allow such a bad thing?"

Somewhere behind these queries is the suspicion that God is apathetic, expressing no passion, feelings or sensitivity to the plights, problems and predicaments of His creation and the creatures He made. Some people view God as a cosmic watchmaker who indeed did create the heavens and earth and all that dwell in them, but then (as one would make a watch, wind it up and allow it to tick-tock on its own) He left it alone without emotional interest or involvement in the ups and downs of the ticks and tocks. Therefore, either He does not know (and therefore is not omniscient) or He knows and does not care (and therefore is without feelings and passion). Either way, we sometimes silently, sometimes verbally, conclude that this sovereign deity is so far removed from the real stuff that happens in the lives of people here on earth that He cannot relate to us—or we to Him.

Without trivializing His majesty, in this book I want to attempt to explore what God reveals to us about His feelings—in

particular, how He expresses His feelings about *us*. Salvation includes God's plan to shape and mold our lives to look like Jesus
the Christ. Paul puts it this way: "For God knew his people in advance, and he chose them to become like his Son" (Rom. 8:29,
*NLT*). This book is a companion to my earlier examination of the
person of God, titled *In His Image*,[1] wherein I ventured into a
study of the physical metaphors used in the Bible to describe
God. For example, when the Bible speaks of "the hand of God,"
it implies that God guides us and protects us; "the eyes of God"
refer to God's all-seeing, all-knowing care and interest in our
lives; and so on. As I stated in my book *In His Image*, "We were
created to live in the image of God. The significance and primary
reason for creation is God's desire to reveal Himself. . . . God
made man in order to show him who He is." In other words, God
wants to be known—in all of His physical, emotional and "personality" attributes and traits.

We must not forget that Jesus was a person with a personality, and that personality reflected the personhood and personality of the Father. The most important trait of God is that He is a
God who loves. More than just an emotional attitude, love is an
action spurred by an emotional attitude. Thus, it is of great comfort when we understand that God loves us through the twists
and turns in our journey through life, through the ups, the
downs and the realities of the emotional roller coaster that char-
acterizes our personal journeys here on earth.

The more we learn about the emotional dimension of the
personhood of God, the more it will help us understand how we
should (and why we do) experience and express the emotions we
all feel. This work is intended to help you learn (as best you can)
to love like God loves, to understand our natural tendency toward anger, jealousy and grieving, and to learn how to handle
such emotions in ways that reflect and honor God. Hopefully, it
will give you a godly affirmation to laugh, rejoice, sing and a
whole range of other emotions that God also expresses.

I pray that through this book you might come to know more
about how important and valuable you are to the God of the uni-

verse, the God of our salvation and the God who passionately cares about you. God has feelings and emotions. And they are all directed at, for and about *us*—His beloved creation.

Kenneth C. Ulmer

**Note**

1. Ken Ulmer, *In His Image* (New Kensington, PA: Whitaker House Publishing Company, 2005).

# Jesus and Whitney...
# Do You Know Them?

Shortly following the 2012 untimely and tragic death of singer Whitney Houston, one of this generation's music icons, the world drifted back to its routine of coming and going and doing business as usual. Other than an occasional spin of one of Ms. Houston's classic performances or songs, for most of the world she will forever remain a sad member of a procession of bright lights who came blazing onto the cultural horizon like shooting stars, only to fade far too soon in the trailing smoke of legend.

As a jarring juxtaposition to Whitney's death and the emotional and passionate outpouring of grief and shock from her family, friends and fans, the tragedy occurred just a few days before Easter of 2012. In fact, as I write this book, just a few weeks after her death, clergy and congregations all over the world are preparing with various degrees of intensity, to commemorate the death, burial and resurrection of Jesus the Christ. From great cathedrals to humble storefronts, plans are being made and solemn ceremonies anticipated for Easter, the biggest day and most sacred season of the Christian calendar. When coupled with the Jewish festival of Passover, it appears that much of the world will (at least for the three days from Good Friday to Easter Sunday) turn its mind, if only for a glance, toward spiritual and pseudo-spiritual matters.

As I write, I glance occasionally at the television screen, which is showing Pope Benedict XVI as he celebrates Papal Mass in Havana (a historic event in itself), marking connection—albeit brief and mostly ceremonial—between the Holy See and the communist country of Cuba. The Holy Father is celebrating the Rite of

Communion, a sacred ceremony full of pageantry, music, color-
ful vestments, and primarily Spanish speaking pilgrims. This holy
service symbolizes the "communion," the oneness, the participa-
tion and sharing in unity of Catholic worshipers with Jesus Christ.
Symbols of the blood and the body of Christ are being distributed
to (and venerated by) an estimated 300,000 in Havana's Revolu-
tion Square and to the Catholic faithful over the airwaves around
the world. Although the earthly head of the Catholic Church leads
the Mass, the spiritual focal point is on Jesus the Christ.

All of which brings me to this query: *What do Jesus and Whitney
have in common?* I suggest the answer is this: both are known the
world over, but both are *known* by very few.

Whitney's funeral was broadcast across the globe to fans and
followers in possibly every nation on earth. The death of this
uniquely talented songstress caught the world off guard. It happened on the weekend of the annual Grammy Award Show in Los
Angeles, where she was scheduled to be the featured singer. I was
with my wife Togetta, my son Kendan and my baby daughter Jes-
sica, in Washington D.C., where I was speaking at Rankin Chapel,
Howard University. As we, along with the world, heard the stunning and painful news that Whitney Houston had suddenly died,
I could scarcely believe it, and my memory flashed back to a few
months earlier, when I had last spoken with her in person.

I knew Whitney. Other than being one of her millions of fans,
I had spoken with her face-to-face on two occasions. The first was
at a worship service held at West Angeles Church of God in Christ
in Los Angeles, pastored by my dear friend Bishop Charles E.
Blake. Whitney was there with another friend, BeBe Winans, among
the thousands of people gathered in the magnificent splendor of
that great cathedral. In the midst of a high time of praise and worship, shouting and rejoicing, BeBe quietly informed me that Whitney wanted me to pray for her. In the midst of the praise, shouting
and celebration, I left the podium and BeBe brought Whitney to
me. After brief introductions, our eyes locked and I felt I was looking into the troubled soul of a gifted, beautiful young woman who
said simply, "Bishop, would you pray for me?" And so I did.

I will never forget the sincerity, sensitivity and purity of Whitney Houston's eyes as she bowed her head, holding my hand as I prayed for her. It was clear that she loved Jesus. From that moment on, I felt the Lord had given me a spiritual connection with this musical gift to the world who sensed her need for something and Someone outside herself, bigger than herself, and more powerful than the demons who trailed her. Not a friendship. Not an intimate relationship of partnership on the journey through the journey of life. Not some commitment to "stay in touch," "give me a call," or "reach out to me"—just a connection in passionate concern as I followed from afar and watched her battle with trials and challenges that so many of us face.

Following that oh so brief time of prayer in West Angeles Cathedral, I would often pray for Whitney, especially whenever I would hear public reports of her personal struggles to hold her life together, position herself for the rebound of her dazzling career, or recover from painful personal relationships.

My second and final personal encounter with Whitney Houston was in May of 2011. At the time, our church, Faithful Central Bible Church, owned the Great Western Forum (former home of the Los Angeles Lakers), which we had been operating as a commercial concert venue for over a decade. In April and May of 2011, Prince (another international music icon) performed there in a series of 15 concerts, 13 of which we sold out. Prince is both a musical and marketing genius. He publicized the concerts as a kind of nightclub hangout, where people would gather each week in the Forum for the flawless renditions of his timeless hits. As Prince would say, "So many hits; so little time." One of the promotional highlights of his performances was that each concert had a surprise element: every night, Prince would announce "unscheduled" guests. The crowd would go wild when the likes of Chaka Khan, Sheila E, Mary J. Blige, Alisha Keys, Foo Fighters or Gwen Stefani "just happened to be in the audience" and made their way to the stage.

The gathering place and unofficial green room for special guests at the Great Western Forum was called the Forum Club. That night the place was packed with VIPs and others. My wife and my son and I were there, awaiting the start of the show, when we were informed that the special guest was going to be Whitney Houston. We were even more surprised when we looked behind us and there, sitting on a couch next to ours was the great diva herself.

"Whitney," I said, reintroducing myself to her, "the last time we saw each other we prayed together."

"Oh, yes, Bishop," she responded, "I remember." We exchanged pleasantries for a brief moment, and then she took my hand and said, "Keep praying for me, Bishop."

That final interchange lasted only a few minutes, and the last thing she said to me was, *Pray for me.* I could tell in her eyes that she was still struggling—and I felt that she *knew* she was struggling. In fact, she did not perform that night. Her prayer request was, in a very strange way, a "help request." I had two very brief encounters with Whitney, and in both she said, "Pray for me." It was the first thing she had ever said to me. And it was the last thing she would ever say to me. The next time I would connect with her would be through pictures, videos and cameos commemorating an all-too-brief, magnificently gifted and anointed life.

I felt like I knew Whitney Houston. But like millions of her fans and acquaintances, I really didn't *know* her.

## The Power of Truly *Knowing*

What are your thoughts about God? Do you envision Him as mysterious, uncaring and unfeeling? Do you think of God as a strict "father figure," void of a sense of humor? Surprisingly, many people do. Yet once we come to understand that God actually expresses a wide range of passion, of emotion, then we can relate to Him on a much more "human" level and begin seeing who He really is in His approach to us. I don't mean "human" in the sense of some common touchy-feely-mushy-buddy kind of relationship that minimizes the honor He is due as Lord, Master, Creator. But I do mean coming to realize that God is relatable and relevant. So, how do God's passions manifest? What does He have "feelings" about? When, why, and how does God express emotions? When we look at the emotions of God, the passions of God, what makes Him feel the way He feels? When we are going through tough times, what does He feel? Does He even feel anything? If so, how does He express those feelings? Do you want to know the answers to these questions?

There is no figure in history who has impacted the world like Jesus Christ. He has been revered, worshiped, honored, celebrated and loved by countless millions throughout the last two millennia. We accept Him, we acknowledge Him, we call Him Savior, we call Him King of Kings and Lord of Lords. We bow down to Him. We cross our bodies with the sign of the cross upon which He died. The world knows Him. Churches, schools, hospitals, ministries both sacred and secular have been birthed, named and exist in His honor. He is known the world over. But I wonder if many truly *know* Him.

Like Whitney, Christ is known, but not truly *known*. And according to His own revelations, if we know Him, then we know His Father. If we see Jesus, we see God. If we know what Christ is like, it gives us insight into who and what the Father is like.

I wish I had *known* Whitney. I wish I had known her personally—her real thoughts, her real struggles, her values, her feelings. I wish I had known who she was, what she was like and how she felt after the performance was over, after the applause had faded and the curtains had come down, after the lights were shut off and her friends had gone home. I wish I had known what drove her, what pulled at her, what motivated her, the limits she set, boundaries she had. I have an iPod filled with her songs. I know her voice. I know her talent. I know her fantastic vocal range. I know her musical versatility. I know her unique ability to "sell" a song through her unique interpretation of lyrics and melody, her intuition, her creativity and passion. I know Whitney . . . but I don't, I didn't ever, and I never will, *know* her. However, I do have a chance to know God. I can't know the Whitney of the stage, but I can know the God of creation.

I join with Apostle Paul, who, speaking of Jesus in Philippians 3:10, said, "I want to know Him." What is God like? How does He feel? What is the emotional side of God? Does He even *have* emotions? How does He really feel about us and about this world He

made? How does He feel about me? How does He feel when I call on
Him? How does He feel when I get in trouble or when I mess up?

There is an old song in the African American tradition that asks
a repetitive question and then answers with a very short answer:

**Question:** "What do you know about Jesus?"
**Answer:** "He's all right!"

The song then goes into a series of questions/descriptions,
each followed by the same response, "He's all right." He's a mother
for the motherless, a father for the fatherless, a lawyer in a courtroom and doctor in the sick room, and so on. But always, the joyous response and testimony is, "He's all right!" As many times as
I have played that song on the keyboard or joined in singing it with
spirited congregations of various sizes, hiding in the anonymity of
the "joyful noise" of those gathered, I have often failed to recognize
the profound short-sightedness of the musical question being
raised. The song asks, "What do you know *about* Jesus?"; not, "Do
you *know* Jesus?"

There is another song from the African American gospel tradition that asks what might be a more appropriate, and certainly a
more profound question. It begins with a testimony and series of
proclamations:

*I know a man from Galilee,*
*If you're in sin, He'll set you free.*
*Oh, Oh, Oh—Do you know Him?*

As with Whitney Houston, I fear that I know far more "about"
Him than I really, truly *know* Him. But I want to know Him. Not
just know about Him, but really *know* Him.

## The Obstacle of Academia

I must admit that I have several obstacles working against my desire to know my God. First, I am hindered by having been trained

and disciplined as a scholar and academician, which can pose a tremendous obstacle to getting to know the real Jesus. Actually, I don't regard myself as either a scholar or academician. Letters behind your name don't always reveal the level of knowledge in your brain! I do consider myself a serious student of the Word, however, and my analytical training in the academy often leads me into the pit of the "paralysis of analysis" (a term I learned from one of my preaching mentors, Dr. A. Louis Patterson).

The second academic obstacle in my quest and desire to know God is the fact that I desire to know a God who is, in a real sense, unknowable.

And third, it is easier, intellectually and factually, to know *about* someone than to truly know them.

Still, I want to know God. But if I am not careful, the very journey that has developed this desire can potentially short-circuit the desire itself.

I have spent most of my life as a student. I have been a seeker of knowledge—and that's a good thing, to a point. The danger I face is that as a student, I have primarily sought information. I have often been like a sponge—even an addict, hooked on the informational transfer process. The problem is that knowing God is not merely about the acquisition of information. Seeking information as a goal can result in the frustrating dilemma of knowing information *about* God, rather than experiencing the inspiration *of* God. It is a hurdle for many a theologian that we can know things about God through the business of the intellectual pursuit of knowledge about Him—something that can blind us to really knowing Him.

I know things about Whitney. I know she was nominated for four Grammys in 1986. I know she won a Grammy for best female pop vocal performance. I know her debut album was on the charts for a record-breaking 14 weeks, sold 25 million copies worldwide, and spun off three number one singles. I know she went back to her gospel roots while branching out into films with her appearance in *The Preacher's Wife,* and her sophomore movie effort after *The Bodyguard* in 1992 (which itself birthed one of the top-selling movie soundtracks of all time). I even know that Whitney loved the Lord and that she saw value in prayer. But I did not *know* Whitney Houston.

Likewise, my training and discipline as a student can result in a knowing *about* God, but does not necessarily bring me into knowledge *of* God where I feel I truly *know* Him—His thoughts, His feelings, His emotions.

## Anthropopathy

A few years ago I wrote a book called *In His Image*, an anthropomorphic (*anthro*, meaning "man," *morph* meaning "form") examination of how God reveals Himself in forms and ideas that we can relate to on a human level. For example, although God is Spirit, we can relate to such terms as "the hand of God," "the eyes of the Lord," "God's heart," and the like—physical terms that help us relate to God. Likewise, as God made humankind in His image, another part of His transferable image is demonstrated in our emotions and feelings.

When we speak in terms of the emotions or feelings of God, it is called "anthropopathy" (*anthropo* meaning "man" and "pathos" or "passion"). Don't let this $9.95 word throw you off. Anthropopathy is when we ascribe to God passions, emotions or feelings that man can relate to—God in the characteristics of human personality. As David R. Blumenthal stated it in his book, *Tselem: Toward an Anthropopathic Theology*: "Since personhood is the core of our being and since we are created in God's image, God must also have personhood. In anthropopathic theology, God has a Face and a real Personal Presence or Personality. To put it formally: personhood, with its expressions as face, presence and personality, is God's and we have that capacity because God has created us in God's image."[1]

In other words, God reveals Himself in passions and feelings like man does. Maybe a better way to put it is that we have feelings and passions because God does. This is one way that He accommodates our desire to understand Him. And we need God's help to understand Him, because with His help, we will find, buried in our sin-tainted human emotional expressions, His sinless paradigm of the same passions. For example, we tend to express angry passion when we're envious; jealous passion when we're selfish; gleeful passion when we've "one-upped" someone; and so forth. We have a range of passionate human responses, feelings and emotions that are based in motives that often are the opposite of what drives the passions of God. However, our earthly motives are often revealed in the same divine method of the Almighty.

So, if God indeed has feelings, then what makes Him feel the way He feels? When we (God's creation) go through certain experiences, what does God feel? In this book, we are going to examine how God feels—His emotions, His *passions*—and how He expresses them. My desire and attempt to study God, to understand and explain God, is an intellectual and philosophical exercise (called *theology*) and, at the same time, a paradoxical enterprise, because I am attempting to understand the incomprehensible, explain the inexplicable, and touch the intangible (see Isa. 55:8). Yet any action, motive and attitude of man will, in some way, be tainted by his imperfection. It is as if God is reaching out to us, but our arms are too short to reach Him. We can't completely comprehend and take a hold of what's in the hand of God. Man then attempts to translate, interpret and communicate in the limitations of His humanity, using earthy words to express heavenly truths.

When God reaches out to us, He must reach down to our level. He made us a little lower than the angels (see Ps. 8:5) but certainly lower than God. He comes down to our capacity to reach Him; to our capacity to understand Him as best we can. He communicates and expresses Himself to us and then we interpret and receive and understand what He says and shows us in language that we can understand.

I have had the honor of speaking in several foreign countries, including South Africa, Ukraine, China and the French-speaking Congo, just to name a few. When I do so, I am assigned an interpreter who translates the message into a language the hearers can understand. He speaks my English words in that local language: Tsutu, Xhosa, Mandarin, Russian or French. When God speaks to us about Himself, we translate God-ideas into man-language. God accommodates our human handicap and limited ability to understand eternal truths.

## The Obstacle of Limited Knowledge

The second handicap to my desire to truly *know* God (after acquisition of knowledge *about* Him) is a theological one. The love of God is released in Christ, but according to Ephesians 4:18-19, this love is beyond understanding; it is unknowable. So, my desire to know this God who *is* love (see 1 John 4:8) and loves with a love that I cannot know is beyond understanding. In other words, I want to know the unknowable. Yet I want to know Him with all my heart. But I am trying to grasp the ungraspable, touch the untouchable. I'm trying to know how God thinks when He has already told me I can't know how He thinks, because He doesn't think like I think. I want to know how He acts, but He has already told me He doesn't act like I act (see Isa. 55:8-9).

It is clear that God *wants* to be known; it says in Ephesians 1:17 that He wants to give us the revelation of Him; and in 1 John 5:20 we read that the Son of God has given us understanding to know Him who is true.

It is also clear that God wants us to obey Him; Yet our obedience is related to knowledge of this unknowable God of ours (see 1 John 2:3-4). My mind, my intellect, cannot fully and completely and totally know Him, but I can know Him more and more. I can never completely know God, but as I draw closer to Him, He draws closer to me (see Jas. 4:8). And the closer I get to Him, the more He reveals who He is and how He is. And maybe that is the point: It is in our ceaseless efforts to know God that we draw ever closer to Him, which is what I believe God wants. Obedience, therefore, is not a position or thing achieved, it is a life that continues to want to know Him, to obey Him and to draw ever nearer to Him.

## The Obstacle of Complacency

A third challenge to my efforts to really know God is complacency. It is much easier to know *about* a person than to know the person.

For example, some of us have experienced the unfortunate and often painful reality of loving someone we don't truly know. But sometimes we don't really want to know the truth of who the other person is. There are also people who draw lines in the sand and will allow us to receive only so much information about them, while guardedly reserving true revelation of who they really are.

One of the comments I most often hear from couples whose love and marriage have disintegrated is, "I really don't know this person." They know what kind of perfume or cologne their spouse wears. They know their favorite food, television show or movie, but they really don't know *the person*. Unfortunately, some people don't want to know any more than they already know, because it's often easier to settle into a comfortable place of knowing "about" rather than truly *knowing*.

Many people make commitments based on a shallow level of emotional "comfort-ability" instead of laboring to truly know the "real" person they love. They try to make themselves satisfied with knowing about the one they love, without really digging into the deeper issues, such as how the person handles the pressures of life and why they handle them in the particular ways they do.

All of this leads me to a very basic question: Can we know God? *Really* know Him?

## To Know God

Paul wrote, "I want to know Christ and the power of his resurrection and the fellowship of sharing in his sufferings" (Phil. 3:10, *NIV*). I am like Paul; I want to know the Lord. I want to take the journey into true knowledge of God. It is a journey valuable more for the direction than the destination. In other words, I recognize and acknowledge that I cannot, and never will fully, totally and comprehensibly know God. However, the value and validity of the disciple's life is to come "follow" Him; to follow hard after Him, drawing ever closer without ever fully arriving.

The word "know," used in Philippians 3:10, suggests "a movement into." It implies a process that begins and continues into

deeper and deeper experience of the revelation. It doesn't mean
we get to a place where we know it all. We are aware that this is a
lifetime journey of personal fellowship and deepening experience
of the nature, character and essence of God. But I want to know
Him to such a degree that it impacts and influences my behavior,
my actions and my interactions with others, my mind, my heart
and my entire being.

I want to be like the angelic living creatures of Revelation 4:8,
who bow continually before the throne of God and do not rest
day or night, saying, "Holy, holy, holy, Lord God Almighty, who
was and is and is to come!" Every time they go down and come up,
they see some new glimmer and revelation of the radiance of the
Living Lord. Like a multifaceted diamond that shows another
facet and dimension of its beauty, you can't look at the exact same
point every time you look, because each time you look, you see
something new.

Likewise, every time you see something new about God, you
make a new declaration about the same dimension: He is holy,
holy, holy. I want to continue to know Him more and more. The
more I know of Him, the more I love Him. The more I love Him,
the more I want to obey Him. The more I want to obey Him, the
more I love Him. The more I love Him, the more I want to know
about Him. The more I know about Him, the more I want to be
like Him. The more I want to be like Him, the more I obey Him.
The more I obey Him, the more I love Him. The more I love Him,
the more I want to know about Him . . . and so on and so on.

I want to know the God who not only created us in His image,
but cares about us after creating us. I am not interested in, nor
could I worship or be attracted to, the concept of God as the
proverbial watchmaker who created a watch and then sat back and
allowed His creation to tick away on its own. I serve the God who
cares about us, a God who has, and expresses, feelings about His
created beings. I don't want to get shackled in the doctrine of impassibility that asserts that God cannot feel. The fact that feelings
are transitory, some theologians would say, disqualifies an unchangeable God from having feelings. Fine. Then that's not my

god. I need the God who cares. I need the God who is emotionally sensitive. I need the God who can relate to my feelings—fleeting though they may be. I need a Savior who understands my emotional pains, fluctuating temptations, joyous triumphs, sorrowful repentance and loving longings for the objects of my love—as flawed as my love may be (particularly in comparison to His).

And I don't want to get confused by all of the theological jargon, intellectual sparring or academic stuff that gets so deep that I can't come back up to an acceptable level of sanity and clarity. *I just want to know Him!*

God says He cares. That's the God I want to know. God says He is jealous. That's the God I want to know. Yet to say that "God cares" is in itself a theological challenge. So, in order to verbalize the dynamics of God in human terms, I have to relate to God in language, terms, words and ideas that I (and humanity) can relate to and comprehend. Fortunately, that is far easier than we think, because God actually does present Himself as emotional—just as we are. In fact, He is the original "emoter" in whose image we are made.

## What Paul Wanted

Part of God's personhood is His emotions, His *passions*. In Philippians 3:10, Apostle Paul says, "I want to share in his sufferings." It is interesting that the word for "suffering" is the word *pascho* (which means "to experience a sensation or impression—usually painful—to feel, passion, suffer, vex").[2] From *pascho* we get our English word "passion."

There is a connection between the sufferings of Christ and the passion(s) of Christ. The same word for "suffering" is used in Acts 1:3, where Jesus showed Himself to His apostles after Calvary. However, it is interesting that the *New International Version, New American Standard Version* and *New King James Version* translate this as His "suffering," and other translations speak of His "death"; whereas the *King James Version* translates it as "passion." Certainly the contexts of both Acts 1:3 and Philippians 3:10 refer to the Calvary event in terms of the physical suffering of our Lord. However,

I suggest that the term "suffering" is multidimensional: it speaks of the physical act of the suffering and pain of the Calvary event, *and* it implies and includes the emotional, psychological mindset of Christ that lay behind the physical manifestation.

The word "suffering" (the *pascho*, the "passion") refers to the *why* behind the *what*. In other words, not only what He did, but also why He did it. It speaks of the passion in the mind of Christ that offered up the body of Christ. Nobody took His life; something in Him willingly laid it down and offered it up in obedience to the Father, who gave Him as an act of love—a *God emotion* (see John 3:16; 10:11,17).

The suffering of Christ includes His state of mind that led Him to Calvary. It was the passion, the emotion, the feelings that led Him, drove Him, compelled Him. I too want to know that kind of God. I want to know that kind of passionate obedience; the passion that is willing to endure all that is required to walk and live in obedience.

When you hear the phrase "the passion play" or "the passion story," or if you saw the 2004 blockbuster movie *The Passion of the Christ,* the word "passion" makes you think about "suffering"—especially the suffering of Christ.[3] Passion and suffering, in the narrowest interpretation, has to do with the experiences of turmoil, pain and struggle that have a physical and mental impact. Remember, this Christ was actually God in the flesh (see John 1:1,14). So this was not only Jesus hanging on the cross, it was God in the flesh hanging on the cross. Thus, God experienced death through His incarnate Son on the cross. God is not dead, but God died!

*Pathema*, passion, is also used to imply affection, feelings and emotions. In other words, Paul knows Jesus hung on the cross, but he wants to know how Christ felt as He hung there, having been nailed down and raised up in exchange for payment of the sins of mankind, from Adam through the last person on earth. What was going through His mind? How did He handle that extreme level of persecution and opposition and anger and judgment and fear directed at Him? In other words, it's not just what happened to Christ, but how what happened to Him impacted His mind. Paul wants to know how Jesus felt—the psychological and emotional impact that the physical suffering caused within Him. Paul's desire is, essentially, to get into the skin, heart and mind of Jesus. *How did this experience mess with God's mind?* That is what Paul is getting at. Because the word "passion" came to mean beyond suffering in a narrow context, and came to mean "intensified emotions."

Paul is not saying that he wants to have actual nails driven through his feet and hands, or thorns crushed into his brow. He's saying that he wants to be able to relate to, to have a certain measure of understanding of, the price Christ paid and the passion that was behind His willingness to pay such a price of pain for us. The emphasis is beyond the experience and focuses on the emotions behind the experience.

When I was a boy, growing up in Mt. Zion Baptist Church in East St. Louis, Illinois, I was told, "Son, don't question God." I used to believe that. Until I carefully read the Calvary account and heard my Lord shouting out in agony on the cross, "My God, My God, why have you forsaken me?" That's a question; and it's a question from the parched lips of a dying Savior on Calvary. Jesus "questioned" God.

So, as I later learned that God saved me to conform me, shape me and mold me to the image His son, my Savior, Jesus, I connected some significant dots in my "Etch A Sketch" life that God is working on as He patiently unscrambles my life and etches the image of Christ into me. I had one of those slap-yourself-on-the-forehead "aha!" moments. If Jesus could have questions, maybe it's okay for me have questions. If, in His humanity, Jesus knew what it was like to be in such a perplexing, problematic place in life that He wondered whether or not God had abandoned Him; and if He shouted out unashamedly in front of His enemies, *God, why have You left me? Why have You abandoned me? Why have You forsaken me?*, then, I concluded, doggone it, if Jesus had questions, then I can have them, too.

And if God could handle Jesus' questions, I knew He could handle my little questions! Calvary put an emotional, hurting, confused Jesus on display. The emotional display of the Master on

Calvary became an encouraging description of the passions of
Christ and continues to help me deal with the emotional junk I
wrestle with every day of my life.

The revelation is that we have a Savior who understands our
emotions because He too has emotions. And if Christ is a Savior
with passions, then God the Father is a God with passions. We
don't have a Savior who cannot be touched or who does not understand what we go through. He can relate to us. He is touchable.
He understands. And since God understands us, Paul says, then *I
want to understand Him*.

Here's where it gets interesting. Paul and Elijah are depicted as
men with "like passions" as ordinary men (see Acts 14:15; Jas.
5:17). This phrase is a combination of the prefix for "like" or
"same" and our root word *pascho* (passion). But it doesn't stop
there. It paints a biblical picture of strong emotion, or passion in
the more classic understanding. This more contemporary idea of
passion is not translated in the *King James Version* of that word. In
Romans 1:26, it is translated as a negative "affection"; in Colos-
sians 3:5, it is "inordinate affection"; and in 1 Thessalonians 4:5,
it is rendered as "lust." Granted, these strong passions or emotions
are relegated to humans; nevertheless, they imply that emotions
can be heightened.[4]

What I want to do in this book is to try to enhance your understanding of the "human-likeness" of God as expressed through
His emotions. (I made up the hyphenated word "human-likeness"
to distinguish between humanity and humanness.) My point is
that the God of the Bible was not human, not even in the sense
that Jesus the Christ was divinity wrapped up in humanity. The
human dimension of the Godhead is firmly and distinctly manifest in Jesus of Nazareth. But my proposition is that the God who
made us in His image made us with some qualities and (as we will
discover) some emotions that have their origin in the personhood
of our Creator.

The feelings that we feel were first felt in the God who made
us with the potential to feel those feelings. Did you get that? God
gave us the ability to be emotional because He is an emotional God.

We will learn about a Creator who is so intimately involved with you—His beloved creation—that, in many ways, He is more like us than we could ever imagine. Or, more accurately, we are more like Him than we could ever imagine. So come with me, if you will, on a journey to discover the passions of our multidimensional, eternal, emotional God. He desires to be known, loved and obeyed by us. To that end, He has chosen to reveal Himself in ways that we, His human creation, can understand, relate to and follow, as a path to the revelation of His ultimate essence of love and holiness.

Yes, I knew Whitney Houston, but I did not really *know* her. I wish I had another chance to personally and intimately know this great artistic gift, this precious creation of a God who passionately loved her. For me, that chance will never come. And I know about the creator God—but that is not enough for me. While I am alive, there is still time to continue to get to learn all about Him. For, my desire is to *really know* Him. I want to know His passions. I want to know how He feels. I want to know Him as an emotional God. Maybe it can help me know myself better. Maybe it can help me understand why I am the way I am. Maybe, just maybe, it will help you, too.

**Notes**
1. David R. Blumenthal, *Tselem: Toward an Anthropopathic Theology of Image,* David R. Blumenthal website. http://js.emory.edu/BLUMENTHAL/image2.html.
2. James Strong, *Strong's Exhaustive Concordance of the Bible* (Nashville, TN: Thomas Nelson, 2003), Greek #3958.
3. *"The Passion of The Christ"* was the highest-grossing Christian-themed movie in history, which was directed by Mel Gibson and starred James Caviezel (Icon Films, 2004).
4. However, it is important to acknowledge that there are negative passions or emotions that could be ascribed to God Himself. This book will not explore this alternate side of an emotional, passionate God, but it cannot be ignored with theological and scriptural integrity. This means that there is an elephant in the theological room of the one who seeks to truly know God. Integrity forces us to acknowledge the reality of a God of emotions (the subject of this book). But that same integrity must also acknowledge that, like our human emotions (which are part of the gift of life given by our sovereign God), God's emotions can be positive as well as negative.

Kenneth C. Ulmer

# 1

# The God Who Loves

*The LORD has appeared of old to me, saying: "Yes, I have loved you with an everlasting love; therefore with lovingkindness I have drawn you."*
JEREMIAH 31:3

When discussing the topic of God's love, one of the first problems we encounter is our tendency to transfer our distorted human concept of love to the biblical concept of God's love. Our image of love tends to portray it as all lovey-dovey, warm and fuzzy; when, in fact, love is multidimensional.

For example, if you've ever been in a bad love relationship with someone—I mean an *un*-anointed, wrong, ungodly relationship—then you probably learned that that's the kind of "love" that will lead you down the wrong path. I'm talking about the kind of love that starts off fine, you can't sleep at night because you are head over heels for the person, and they're always on your mind. Then it goes like a Bell curve: things reverse and you go on a roller coaster ride of misery and regret. You still can't sleep at night and you still can't get them off your mind, but for completely different reasons.

That is the result of mankind's distorted concept of "love."

When I consider ministry to this generation, I see a troubling pattern concerning love and commitment that is all out of whack. Because of what we've been taught and told about love, our idea of love has been distorted to the point where few people understand what love really is. The perception of love that has been painted by the media—movies, magazines, the internet, advertising, television—portrays a grotesque imitation of "love" that is not from God. This is because the world is trying to frame and shape its own concept of love, rather than adopt God's concept and model of love. The world's perspective of love always defaults to the fallen nature of man.

These days, so-called "love" is a temporary kind of emotion that does not grasp concepts like *commitment* and *unconditional*. In stark contrast, God's concept of love includes commitment, it involves permanence, and it is unconditional. It does not trade up, trade across, trade down, or trade at all. It is a state of permanence, a condition of the heart that does not waver. It simply *is*. When God says He loves you with an everlasting love, He is saying that He is committed to loving you, period. No matter what.

My fear is that today's and tomorrow's generations know only two things about integrity, character, holiness, consistency and commitment: little and nothing. Those words and concepts sound like speaking in tongues to most people these days. That is why we must go beyond man's idea of love to God's concept of love and make a decision that His is the kind of love we want to emulate. Because the moment we decide to settle for less, we have opened a door that takes us in an entirely different direction—one that leads only to dissatisfaction and instability.

The bottom line is that man's love will let you down and disappoint you. That is the reality of horizontal human love. That's not a criticism; it's simply the truth. If you have ever been in love, you know what I'm talking about. Whereas, God's love will never fail you, no matter what you're going through, no matter how you feel, no matter what the enemy whispers in your ear. No matter how bad things look, God's love never fails.

Have you ever felt like turning back? Ever felt like things just aren't working out for you, no matter how hard you try, so it's time to give up and try something else? When you're really honest with yourself, have you ever felt you've done your best and your best must not be good enough? Have you felt like the Lord heard everybody but you asked God for maybe one too many things, and now you've gotten to the place where you plead, "I don't ask for much, God . . . but could You at *least* do this one thing for me?"

I have sometimes felt as if God must have chosen the wrong person to handle what He assigned me to do, because it sure isn't something that I feel I can adequately handle. When God looks at my life and sees what I'm going through, I wonder how He feels—not just what He does about it, but how He actually *feels*.

In this chapter, we're going to look through the eyes of the prophet Jeremiah at the emotions and passions of God and the expression of His feelings.

The book of Jeremiah is most often looked at as a book of prophecy and history. It's a biography in which more is revealed of the life of this prophet than any other prophet, major or minor. The book is also a "chiasm." The word *chiasmus* (or *chiasm*) is a rhetorical structure that has repetition on both ends and a peak at the middle. The book of Jeremiah is a chiastic revelation that begins with judgment, is held together with the hinge of hope, and closes with judgment. Chapters 2 through 28 are about judgment; chapters 29 through 33 are about hope; and chapters 34 to the end of the book are also about judgment. The key verse is Jeremiah 31:3. "The LORD has appeared of old to me, saying, 'Yes, I have loved you with an everlasting love.'" Everything said before this leads up to this verse, and everything said through the end of this book flows from this verse. Everything that is said from the beginning of the book leads to God's words, "Yes, I have loved you." Judgment, judgment; trials, trials; problems, problems—*but I love you*. So the entire revelation is in the truth, the foundation and the fact of the everlasting love of God.

The essence of the emotions, the character, the very nature of God, is that He is love (see 1 John 4:8 and 16). Not simply that He does love, but that He *is* love. Therefore, the foundation for the examination of God's passion, God's driving emotion, begins with the revelation that the character and person of God is His everlasting *love*. From that one emotion, all of His other emotions passionately flow. He loves us with a protective, unconditional, everlasting love that never fails. Don't miss that. Every other emotion we examine in this book is related to, and is an outworking of, God's everlasting love.

The Hebrew word for *everlasting* is *'owlam*, which is related to the word for *eon*; it's a word that means "beginning and no end." God is not saying to the prophet, "I love you," but, "I have *always* loved you"—past, present and forevermore. God knew Jeremiah before he was born. He loved Jeremiah before he was even born. *I have always loved you*. It's the same way God loves us. We read in Jeremiah 3:15, "I will give you shepherds according to My heart, who will feed you with knowledge and understanding." God loves us like a shepherd who cares for His sheep.

Have you ever thought about the fact that God loves you enough to bring you to the point of reading about Him at this very moment? I don't say that arrogantly. Realize the connection: the fact that you are reading about God, attending a church, going to a Bible study, all flow out of His love for you.

Your pastor wants you to grow and be fed with knowledge and with understanding. For this season of your life, God has planted you in your church. The fact that He has planted you in that house is a demonstration of His love for you. As the good Shepherd, He wants His sheep to grow.

There ought to be some stuff you can handle today that would have knocked you down last year. God is growing you. There's not a person in any Bible preaching church who is there by accident. We are where we are by God's love for us.

## Love Drives God's Passion

In Jeremiah 3:11-14, we read, "Then the LORD said to me, 'Backsliding Israel has shown herself more righteous than treacherous Judah. Go and proclaim these words toward the north, and say: "Return, backsliding Israel," says the LORD; "I will not cause My anger to fall on you. For I am merciful," says the LORD; "I will not remain angry forever. Only acknowledge your iniquity, that you have transgressed against the LORD your God, and have scattered your charms to alien deities under every green tree, and you have not obeyed My voice," says the LORD. "Return, O backsliding children," says the LORD; "for I am married to you. I will take you, one from a city and two from a family, and I will bring you to Zion." ' "

How does God love you? God loves you like a parent loves a stubborn child. Over and over I will use the rhetorical device called a *simile*. A simile is a figure of speech that compares two things. They are compared not by telling what they are, but by telling what they are like. This is a grammatical construct that says, "I can't really put into words what this is exactly, but I can tell you what it is like." In a similar way, we can't really describe the "what" of God's love; the best we can do is tell what His love is like. God loves *like* a parent who loves a stubborn child.

The prophet Jeremiah uses the term "backsliding" more often in this book than it appears in any other Scripture. God refers to these "children" as those who have turned from Him and have rebelled from their Father. God loves you like a father of a disobedient child. Have you ever noticed how some parents allow their children to treat them, yet they still love their children? I'm talking about parents who have sacrificed and worked hard for their children, yet their children are ungrateful.

Jeremiah 3:20 describes this love of God another way: "Surely, as a wife treacherously departs from her husband, so have you dealt treacherously with Me, O house of Israel." God loves you like a spouse who never gives up loving an unfaithful mate.

In this verse, Jeremiah again uses the word "backsliding." He speaks of a relationship between a husband and wife in which one of them has backslidden. It's a picture of someone who gets married but continues to live like they're single. It's a picture of a spouse who has turned away from his mate, yet she calls for him to come back. The image is of a spouse who is an adulterer, backsliding and running around acting like a whore. Jeremiah paints a picture of a lover who has been betrayed. He uses the phrase "going after other gods," yet He says, "I still love you." Watch how God loves: "Return, backsliding Israel . . . I will not cause My anger to fall on you. For I am merciful . . . I will not remain angry forever" (v. 12). This is a love that begs for a return. *I know you've betrayed me. I know you've cheated. I know you've committed adultery. I know you've walked away from me. But return, because I'm merciful.* He says, My anger won't last long. The first revelation is, "I am angry, and I deserve to be angry. But come on back. My anger won't last long."

I was talking to a young lady awhile ago who found out she was pregnant and hadn't told her father yet. "What are you going to do?" I asked her.

"I don't know," she said. "But when I tell him, he's going to be mad."

"He deserves to be disappointed after all he went through to sacrifice for you," I replied. "But his anger won't last forever."

God too is a father. He'll get angry and upset with us when we sin—and He's justified for His anger. But God is also merciful, because He loves us. You may as well get used to the use of interchangeable words like mercy and grace and love; because the more you do, the more you will see that they are all parts of the many dimensions of the love of God. God says, in Jeremiah 31:3, "I have loved you with an everlasting love. Therefore, with lovingkindness I have drawn you." It's a picture of someone pulling with a rope. The reason this verse blows my mind is because I think back on the places He has had to pull me out of. He doesn't tug too much on Sunday mornings, but on nights like Friday and Saturday, He does a drawing ministry. No one is around after the benediction when you're in the wrong place at the wrong time with the wrong people. But He is always drawing us (sometimes yanking us) to Himself, loving us to Himself.

A few years ago, I was in Bermuda watching a man as he fished. When he cast his line out with the long pole, I noticed that he would pull and then rest a little while . . . pull . . . rest a little. It dawned on me that between the pulls, the fish were still swimming, thinking they were getting away. But the man was tugging and pulling, tightening up, reigning the fish in gradually so that the fish thought it was getting away, but every time it wiggled, it had less wiggle room, because the fisherman was gradually drawing them in. I thought about the times that I've tried to wiggle. The times I've tried to go another direction, but by the love of God, He drew me to Himself.

If you get nothing else out of what God wants to tell you through this book, then get this: GOD LOVES YOU. I know that seems elementary and redundant. But God's Word tells us, "We know that the Son of God has come and has given us an understanding, that we may *know* Him who is true" (1 John 5:20, emphasis added). It's one thing that He loves us, but it's another thing that we may *know*, in our spirit—deep in our heart, in our very bones—that He loves us.

Have you ever been in love with somebody secretly, and the moment they caught your eye, you started breathing faster? It doesn't matter that you love them—until they know. I am absolutely amazed at how much God loves me. I think the reason I'm amazed is because He knows all about me, yet He *still* loves me! Some people love me, but they don't really know me. Others know me and can't stand the ground I walk on. But the reason it's so amazing with God is that He loves me with an everlasting love, a no-matter-what love. When I was too foolish to call on Him, when I was so far out there I didn't even want Him to remind me that He was calling me, He loved me. I'm amazed at how He loves me. At how He would cast His line to the depths of me and draw me by His love, draw me with His love.

In human terms, love is God's most powerful emotion of all: love drives His passion.

*Who shall separate us from the love of Christ? Shall tribulation,*
*or distress, or persecution, or famine, or nakedness, or peril, or sword? . . .*
*I am persuaded that neither death nor life, nor angels nor principalities*
*nor powers, nor things present nor things to come, nor height nor*
*depth, nor any other created thing, shall be able to separate us from the*
*love of God which is in Christ Jesus our Lord.*
ROMANS 8:35,38-39

## REFLECTION QUESTIONS

1. What is the key difference between an anthropomorphic examination of God and anthropopathy?

2. What is the primary motive for God's passion?

Kenneth C. Ulmer

3. Give one example of why God might permanently withdraw His love from you?

4. In what ways have you have tried to wiggle away from God's love but found that He drew you back to Himself?

5. What is the primary difference between human love and God's love?

# 2

# The God Who Is Jealous

*For you shall worship no other God, for the* LORD,
*whose name is Jealous, is a jealous God.*

EXODUS 34:14

Everything God does—all of His dealings with us, His created beings—will always be connected to His everlasting love for us. Yet, according to the passage above, we find that this God who loves us so much is also a jealous God. Romans 5:5 tells us, "God has poured out his love into our hearts" (*NIV*). The Greek word for "pour" is *ekcheo*, which means "to pour forth" or "to bestow"; the phrase literally means God has poured into us His everlasting love. And now we discover from Exodus 34:14 that this God who has poured His love into us is a *jealous* God. In fact, His very name is Jealous.

This presents a challenge to us, because for most of us, jealousy is not a positive emotion, and the word "jealous" is usually used in a negative way. In fact, Galatians 5:20 lists jealousy among the works of the flesh, the acts of the sinful nature. If jealousy is an act of the flesh, and if it is seen as a negative emotion, then how is it that a Holy God can be a jealous God?

The key has to do with this principle of jealousy. The root of the Hebrew word for jealousy is a word that means "to become darkened red." It speaks of a process by which a red hue is developing. The idea is that something is changing; it had been at one level of color, but is now becoming a darkened red. The New Testament word for jealous means "to boil," "to be heated" or "overheated." It's a word that indicates hot passion, boiling fervor, something that is inflamed to the point of becoming a reddened,

Kenneth C. Ulmer

glowing hue. It is an idea of a dynamic passion—one that even our loving God has.

The word "jealousy" is used almost exclusively in relation to God. The most common usage of the idea of jealousy when applied to God is seen in the picture and context of the relationship between a husband and wife. It is the language of the feeling in a husband of exclusive right to his wife. For example, God is wedded to Israel and claims exclusive rights to her loyalty. Violation of this loyalty is depicted as adultery and becomes the provocation of God's jealousy (see Deut. 21:16, 21; 1 Kings 14:22; Ps. 78:58; Ezek. 8:3; 16:38,42; 23:25; 36:5; 38:19).

Thus, jealousy is not necessarily a negative emotion. When used in the context of God, it is a passionate desire to possess what He already has, what is already His. The focus is on what is already rightfully ours that we don't want to lose; not on what someone else has that we want.

Now let's take a closer look at two words that are associated with jealousy: "zeal" and "envy."

## Zeal

*Zelos*, the Greek word for jealousy, is the word from which we get our English word zeal. God is seen as zealously jealous in His passionate desire to possess, to hold onto, and to receive the loyal devotion of His people—His bride—which He claims as His divine possession. Godly zealous jealousy, then, is a passionate desire to possess or to hold onto something that is already yours. It's an emotion of passionate possession that desires to protect, to possess, to hold on to.

God is a "consuming fire" against all evil both within and without Israel, but full of zeal on behalf of the salvation of His people (see Deut. 4:24). The operative idea is that this jealous zeal is toward "His" people—the people He possesses. The jealous nature of God is legitimized by His possession, His ownership, of His people. We belong to Him. We are His people. He purchased and redeemed us (see Deut. 7:8; 1 Cor. 6:20; Heb. 9:12). He is jealous for those whom He already possesses. The requirement of the covenant love that God has for His people demands absolute devotion with no allowance for idolatrous flirtations, adulterous flings or sharing of one's worship and adulation of anyone or anything but God. God is zealous in His love for us. He refuses to be a part-time lover!

The problem with zeal in humans is that it can go either way: it can take on a negative dimension or it can take on a positive one. I believe when zeal is positive, it becomes justifiable, or godly, jealousy. When zeal has a negative motive, it becomes *envy*.

## Envy

Envy\en-vē [Gk *zēlos*] 1: MALICE 2: painful or resentful awareness of an advantage enjoyed by another, joined with a desire to possess the same advantage.[1]

Envy, on the other hand, is a passionate desire to have and possess what *someone else* possesses or to experience what *someone else* has experienced. The Greek word for envy is *phthonos*, which *Strong's Dictionary* defines as "to feel ill-will or spite for something or someone."[2] When the word envy is used in Scripture, it is used only in connection to man, never in reference to God. This is because to envy means to desire something that someone else has, and God could never be envious of something that someone else has, because the earth is the Lord's and the fullness thereof (see Ps. 50:12 and 1 Cor. 10:26 and 28). It's all God's anyway—there's no reason for envy.

Envy can kill you. Whether it is envy over someone else's job, someone's spouse, someone else's career, someone else's body or physique, it does not matter. Proverbs 14:30 says, "A sound heart is life to the body. But envy is rottenness to the bones." It suggests a decay that progresses even into your bones.

Feelings of envy due to what someone else has or is or does will also kill your spirit. It will kill your gratitude for who and what you are. It will kill your appreciation for your own gifts and for what God has done for you. It will kill your perspective of seeing that what they have cost them a price; and you may not be willing to pay the price they paid for what they have. Envy eats away at the life force in you. Envy makes you bitter and irritable. It makes you mean, nasty and angry. It is a rottenness that spoils your spirituality and your focus on the things of God. King Saul, who was envious of young David, is a stark example of what envy can do to a person. As depicted in 1 Samuel 18–31, envy cost Saul his very life.

I know a man who pastors a 35-year-old church of a few dozen people. He resents other pastors and preachers who have larger ministries. He's the only man I know who gets up every week and fusses at folks who aren't there—and they can't even hear him (well maybe not *every* week, but you get my drift). He has been bitter for the last 30 years. Envy will poison your personality; and the bitterness that can result from wanting what you do not have will prevent you from getting what you really want.

## It's About Covenant Love

When God says He is jealous, it is an illustration of the Divine Mind—a description that only describes God. God's jealousy is not only part of His name, but in relation to us, His creation, it is also His nature. Thus, the presupposition of jealousy is that it is in the framework and the context of a relationship of committed covenant love. Exodus 34:14-17 describes a covenant love:

> (For you shall worship no other god, for the LORD, whose name *is* Jealous, is a jealous God), lest you make a covenant with the inhabitants of the land, and they play the harlot with their gods and make sacrifice to their gods, and one of them invites you and you eat of his sacrifice, and you take of his daughters for your sons, and his daughters play the harlot with their gods and make your sons play the harlot with their gods. You shall make no molded gods for yourselves.

When God tells us not to make a covenant with any other gods, He sees His people as being in a covenant relationship with Him (see

Ezek. 34:31). The violation of that relationship is what God describes as "whoring after" other gods. God is saying that because of the covenant relationship we have made with Him, we cannot develop or pursue such a relationship with other gods, for to do so is to disrupt the very covenant, the very unity, we have with our Creator.

In Jeremiah 3:14, God says He is married to Israel. If I am part of a church, and Church is the bride of Christ, then God says that because of my covenant relationship with Him, He is jealous for me. He is expressing *justified possessiveness*. Justified because we're in a covenant relationship: Ezekiel 34:31 established that we are God's people and He is our God. And since we are His people and He is our God, He has a justifiable right to be jealous when we go whoring around with other gods. The key is the presupposition of a covenant commitment relationship that justifies possessiveness.

For example, just as God says He is our God and we are His people, a husband says to his wife, "You are my lady, and I'm your man." And a wife says to her husband, "I am your wife, and you are my husband." They are justified in being jealous for keeping their covenant commitment exclusive to one another—they don't want anyone else mixing in with the intimacy and exclusivity of their relationship.

It's similar to when, many years ago, Princess Diana was being interviewed after she and Prince Charles had separated, and (in a rough paraphrase of the conversation) she was asked by the interviewer, "Do you think you would have wanted to be Queen?"

"No," Diana replied. "I don't think I would have liked being Queen."

"Why not?"

"Because there were those who didn't want me to be in that position," she responded.

"And how did that affect your marriage to Prince Charles?"

"It didn't have much of a chance," Diana answered with a demure smile, "because there were too many people in the marriage."

She had made a commitment with Prince Charles, yet too many people got involved in their covenant marriage. That was justified jealousy on the part of Princess Diana.

God too can be jealous—justifiably possessive—of His people. Genesis 2:24 says, "Therefore, a man shall leave his mother and father and be joined to his wife. And they shall become one flesh." Two have now committed to become one, and there is now a new entity, because those two individuals came together to become *one* flesh, one new person, the covenant combination of two formerly separate individuals. Any intrusion between the two now violates the oneness of the covenant.

When there is more than one in the covenant relationship, there are too many people involved in it. Therefore, it is justifiable that the two who have become one should be jealous for the other one, because they are now one whole person. Violation of such a commitment is so serious that, in terms of punishment, adultery can be seen as just as significant as murder, because breaking the marriage covenant both kills something that was alive and tries to replace it with the introduction of a third party into the mix.

When we cheat, we have violated a commitment. That violation kills the oneness and unity of the relationship, which is why we cannot cheat and come back and act like everything is the same. It's the same idea as when we have the Holy Spirit inside of us, as a part of us, after we ask and receive Christ into our heart as Lord of our life. If we bring any other "god" into the mix, we have violated the unique oneness that the joining of the two created.

In Joshua 24:19, Joshua was trying to explain to the people what it really meant to follow God: "But Joshua said to the people, 'You cannot serve the LORD, for He is a holy God. He is a jealous God; He will not forgive your transgressions nor your sins.'" Joshua wasn't telling them not to worship God; He was telling them that they needed to understand what they were getting into when they made a covenant commitment with God. Joshua's words are telling us that when we enter into a covenant relationship with God, we can't do the sorts of things we used to do and still try to worship Him, because God is a holy God, a jealous God, and He won't put up with our fooling around and sinning.

# More Than a Casual Commitment

Being in covenant with God is not a plaything. You don't just casually make a commitment with God. If you do, you don't understand what kind of God you're getting connected to or what kind of lover God is. He doesn't like to be taken for granted. Don't make a casual commitment to Him and then back off. Because God is a jealous God. When you get into a relationship with Him, He takes it seriously, because He takes love seriously.

In your personal life, you might need to develop such a reputation that when someone chooses to be with you, they'll know it will be serious business. They might need to know that there are certain things you won't put up with, boundaries you will not cross, behavior you will not tolerate. And if they're looking for someone who plays around on the side, then you need to tell them to move on, because you don't play that game. You're not looking for just a casual date—you're too serious for that. God says, Don't *mess around, because you are not getting a pass to go in and out, back and forth, off and on with Me*. He is a jealous God who does not put up with any insincerity or lack of full commitment.

One reason so many people put up with so much dishonesty in a relationship is because they keep allowing so much dishonesty from the other person. One of the challenges I see in marriages today is that some spouses are not serious about the covenant commitment. Marriage is not an extended date. It is a commitment that justifies possessiveness. And if you do make a commitment to be in a relationship, the person with whom you are in that relationship is justified in saying, "I'm yours and you are mine." I'm jealous over my wife, because for more than 30 years we've made a commitment. She is as justified in being jealous over me as I am over her.

Now, recognition that God is a jealous God is a positive thing. It should produce zeal in our lives for Him. It ought to provoke us, encourage us, motivate us to love God the way He loves us. It should make us just as possessive of Him. We ought to be so sensitive about our relationship with Him, so caring, so possessive and so passionate in our desire to keep that relationship in order, that we are zealous for Him.

When I realize how much God loves me, it ought to motivate me to love Him more. When I realize how much God has done for me and has cared for me, it ought to be the very motivation to draw me closer to Him. There ought to be some things that I will not do, because of who I am in God. There ought to be a line that I draw in my character and in my walk that I refuse to cross, because to do so would violate and shame and leave a negative impression on the very God I say I serve. We need to have a zeal for goodness, for righteousness. We should want to live a holy life, to never lower the bar or compromise our integrity, because we reflect upon the God who jealously loves us.

I am gripped by my commitment to my wife, for example, because to violate it would make her look bad. It would hurt her. I'm so jealous of our relationship that I can't mess around with it. I have to draw some lines. I have to set some boundaries. I can't step over it, I can't toy with it, I can't flirt with stuff over there. Because I'm jealous and I'm zealous about the commitment this woman has made to me and that I have made to her. She has a justified possessiveness. I ought to be that zealous for God, because He is that jealous for me.

## Zealous for God

In Revelation 3:15 and 16, God tells us what He thinks of us when we are not zealous in our jealousy for Him: "I know your works, that you are neither cold nor hot. I could wish you were cold or hot. So then, because you are lukewarm, and neither cold nor hot, I will vomit you out of My mouth."

It's as if you are at a coffee shop with a nice, hot cup of coffee. You put the cup to your lips, expecting a hot beverage, but as it hits your tongue, it's room temperature, and you spit it out and say, "Blah!" God says, "You make me spit you out. You are neither hot nor cold; you are neither passionate nor zealous." Some coffee houses and coffee shops sell iced coffee, so they have both hot and cold coffee. But no one sells lukewarm coffee. Very few things are as repulsive as coffee that is neither hot nor cold. It makes you want to spit it out.

That's what the Lord is saying. "At least be one or the other—hot or cold—because this lukewarm commitment of yours is making Me sick to My stomach. You're not committed to Me. You won't express your exclusive desire and love for Me. And on the other hand, you won't leave Me alone." He wants us to *get off the fence*. He wishes we were either hot or cold, instead of just trying to play Him. Hot enough to stay in the crowd but too cold to make a commitment. Hot enough to date Him, but too cold to marry Him. Lukewarm, room temperature, blah. "You make Me want to spew you out," God says.

How should we respond with the love of a jealous God like that? God says in Revelation 3:19, "As many as I love, I rebuke and I chasten. Therefore be zealous and repent." *Heat up your love*, God is saying. *Be passionate again about your love for Me.* The amazing thing about God is that He has admitted that their love has been tainted, that they don't love Him the right way. Yet, He says He still loves them. Why? Because, as He says in Jeremiah 31:3, "I have loved you with an everlasting love." *So repent, change your direction and come back to Me, so I can stop being jealous.*

There is a great movie called *Atonement*, which has several scenes where actress Keira Knightley is talking to the man she loves—a man who has been abused, lied about, falsely accused and sent to jail. Right when he feels like giving up, right when he's losing it, she looks him in the eye and lovingly says, "Come back to me, come back to me, come back to me." That's the kind of love God has for you. You've been through all sorts of heartaches and hard breaks, and you're ready to walk away from God permanently. But God says, *Come on back. Come back to Me. Repent and be zealous. Stoke up the fires again. Come back to Me.*

God looks into your spiritual eyes with His eyes of love and says, *Come back. You put someone or something else in My place. You left Me and went chasing someone who ended up hurting you, a false god who betrayed you. But come back to Me. You've gone after other lovers and you walked away and violated your commitment to Me. But come back to me. I don't care how bad it was out there, I don't care what happened out there, I don't care what you did, I don't care how far away you got, I don't care how far down you fell, I don't care how bad you missed the mark. Come back to Me. Repent. Change your direction. Turn around. Come back.*

If you have drifted away from God and your love for Him has gone cold, you can humbly call upon Him as a jealous God who is saying to you, *Repent.* He loves you with an everlasting love. If you have violated your love covenant with God, if you have disobeyed Him, if you have walked away from Him, then simply realize that He loves you enough to say, *Come back to Me.* He is drawing Himself to you. He is a jealous God for your committed love. He wants you back.

*I, the LORD your God, am a jealous God.*
EXODUS 20:5

# REFLECTION QUESTIONS

1. What are some examples that show jealousy is not necessarily a negative emotion.

2. What is the difference between zeal and envy?

3. Why is God never envious?

4. What is one example of an experience in your life when you felt or expressed jealousy? What was the outcome of that experience?

**Notes**
1. *Merriam-Webster's Collegiate Dictionary* (New York: Merriam-Webster, 2008), s.v. "envy."
2. James Strong, *Strong's Exhaustive Concordance of the Bible* (Nashville, TN: Thomas Nelson, 2003), Greek #5355.

# The God Who Becomes Angry

*God is a just judge, and God is angry with the wicked every day.*
PSALM 7:11

What makes you mad? What ticks you off? What pushes your anger button?

I asked this question of several newlyweds in my congregation one Sunday morning, and the answers ranged from "Not listening," to "A lack of affection," to "Messing up the money." It's interesting that in many love relationships, one of the last things you learn about the person you love is what makes them angry, what their "hot buttons" are, the things that really tick them off. The reality is, if you're in any significant relationship, then at one point or another, someone will become upset. Unfortunately, those are the things people often learn late in a relationship.

When I meet with couples who are about to get married, one of the questions I ask them is, "Tell me, what do you two argue about?" I always get a little nervous with this question, because if they reply, "Oh, we never argue," then that means that they have an extremely unique and very shallow relationship. Because the truth is, in every substantive relationship, at some point there will be conflict, even to the level of someone getting angry. More times than not, it means they have not been together long enough, or they have not ventured into the camouflaged places of fear, pain, and vulnerability in their mate.

Very few of us are immune to becoming angry. You might think, *But I'm very even-keeled—I don't get upset that much.* However, for the most part, in each of us there is an emotion or a feeling that sometimes expresses itself in overt irritation. We each have boundaries, sensitive areas, things that are delicate to us. And when those things are violated or those lines are crossed, the reality of our humanness is that we can get upset. Most of us handle it pretty well when others become angry. But things change when we move the issue of anger into our vertical relationship with God. In other words, if you're upset with me and don't want to talk to me, I can handle that. But to think that God might be mad at me puts the topic on a whole new level. Is it possible that God could be so angry with me that He might not even speak to me? Absolutely. And the reason is because our tendency toward anger is due to the fact that God made us that way; and the catch is that He made us *in His own image*. That means that the emotions and feelings we have (particularly those that are fragile and can be hurt) can result in our expressing anger. This is simply a reflection of the fact that we are modeled after God Himself. So, just as you and I are emotional beings, God too is an emotional, passionate Being.

However, to ascribe to this holy God the emotion of anger does not sit well with some people, because there is a reluctance to acknowledge that this God, who is the God of love—who *is* love incarnate—could also be a God of anger. In an attempt to suggest that God could not possibly be this or that "kind of God," many people resort to what is called a "theodicy," which is an attempt to vindicate or validate the person of God, to defend His character or protect His image. Many people try to explain away God's perceived "negativities" because they don't want people to think or talk "that way" about Him. Other people simply revise their theology. They acknowledge that maybe God feels or expresses anger, but they try to explain it away: "Well, sure, the Bible says that. But what it really means is something else." It's an attempt to revise our theology, to redress God, to not be faced with the examination of the possibility that God shares many attributes with His created beings, including those that we perceive as negative. Still other people simply disregard any "negative" attributes of God—completely ignoring the reality that we are emotional, passionate beings who God made in His own image. And this God who is an emotional God, can also express the emotion of anger. God sometimes gets *ticked off*.

There are at least seven Hebrew synonyms for anger, and at least two in Greek. In fact, there are more words, texts, passages, stories and narratives that express God's *wrath*, *fury* and *anger* in the Bible than words that speak of God's love. Anger is imply an emotion that is a part of the personality of God.

Interestingly, one of the words used for "anger" is the same root word for "nose." It speaks of someone who is so angry that they breathe hard. Have you ever seen somebody get so mad that their breathing becomes hard and their nose starts flaring? That's one of the pictures that the Bible paints of God when He is angry. It's a furious wrath. When the Bible talks about God breathing and God allowing the wind to blow, it is speaking of God breathing out so hard that the wind of His breath becomes judgmental. There are also passages that talk about the fiery wrath of God, or God flaming with rage. The reality is that God, who is a God of love, is also a God who can get angry.

## God's Love Versus God's Holiness

In the previous chapter, we learned that our God of love is also a God who can become jealous, which stems from His desire to protect and to possess what belongs to Him. God's jealousy is a function of God's *love*; it's the result of a violation of *what God owns*. His anger, on the other hand, is a function of God's *holiness*, because the source of His anger is *our sin and disobedience*, which is a violation of *who God is*.

God is in a category by Himself—holy, separate, sanctified. One of the reasons it is important for us to study the idea of why God becomes angry is because it will highlight just how serious He is about sin. Sin is what God responds to in anger and wrath, for it violates the very essence of this God who loved us before He even created us.

Let's take a look at three things that make God angry.

## 1. A Complaining Spirit

> Now when the people complained, it displeased the LORD,
> for the LORD heard it, and His anger was aroused. So the
> fire of the LORD burned among them, and consumed some
> in the outskirts of the camp (Num. 11:1).

As the verse above shows, God becomes angry at a complaining spirit, an attitude of ingratitude. The people whined about what they didn't have; they complained about what they missed. Their kvetching went up to God, and He became upset because of it. Notice something interesting in the passage above: these were people who had already been blessed, who had already come through the Red Sea and had been delivered from Egypt, yet they were complaining. A complaining, disgruntled spirit angers God.

What do you complain about? What don't you have that you're upset with God about not having? I know people who have turned away from God because He didn't give them what they wanted or thought they were entitled to have. I know people who have abandoned God because He didn't do what they wanted when they wanted Him to do it.

Rather than complaining, we need to learn to live in a spirit of thanksgiving, where we realize that things may not be what we wished they were, but thank God they're as good as they are, because many people have it much worse—and many of them don't complain about it. For the believer, all that we do must be done with a spirit of gratitude, a sense of contentment that appreciates and doesn't complain.

## 2. A Hindering Spirit

And in the greatness of thine excellency thou hast overthrown them that rose up against thee: thou sentest forth thy wrath, which consumed them as stubble (Exodus 15:7).This verse says that God sent forth His wrath. *Wrath* is "activated anger." God's anger and wrath rose up against the Egyptians when He saw their injustice against the Jewish nation in trying to prevent the Israelites from being all He called them to be.

Notice the pattern:

- God feels jealousy when that which belongs to God is taken from Him.
- God becomes angry about the situation.
- The people begin to complain about it.
- God's wrath kicks in and He does something about that which angered Him.

God *feels*, He *becomes angry*, the people *complain*, He *acts*. The context of the Exodus passage above is the story of the Israelites' deliverance out of Egypt. The goal of the Egyptians was to keep the Hebrews in bondage and therefore prevent them from receiving the promises and destiny of God. God's anger arose because of that injustice—a hindering.

God becomes angry when anything or anybody tries to prevent you from becoming all He has called you to be, or when anything seeks to destroy or distort the destiny God has placed in your life. God had ordained that the Hebrews would move into the promises. Yet the goal of the enemy in Egypt was to prevent them, to keep them in bondage so they might miss their destiny. Likewise, God rises up against injustice that would prevent you from being all He has called you to be. He rises up against a system that wants to stop you from being the success He wants you to be. What is trying to hold you back? What excuse are you using to prevent yourself from being all that God has ordained for you? Whatever it is, God is angry against it. Whatever seeks to keep you in bondage or stunt your success, God rises up in anger against.

That same passage, Exodus 15:3, says that God is a warrior. God's love for you causes Him to go to war against anything in your life that would hold you back from being the person of destiny He called you to be. Whatever it is that is trying to hold you back, whatever habit, whatever mindset that has you literally in bondage, God becomes a man of war against it, rising up at anything (including your own sin, actions, or inactivity) that tries to stop what He wants in you, from you, and for you.

Kenneth C. Ulmer

We've examined the complaining spirit and the hindering spirit. Now let's look at one more spirit that causes God to get angry.

### 3. A Disobedient Spirit

> So the LORD became angry with Solomon, because his heart had turned from the LORD God of Israel, who had appeared to him twice (1 Kings 11:9).

There are several layers of revelation in this passage. First of all, God became angry with Solomon. In our common vocabulary, we would say, "God was mad at him." Solomon was His boy—David's son, the king, leader of God's nation. He was also the wisest, wealthiest man who had ever lived. Yet, God became angry with Solomon because his heart had turned from God even after He had appeared to him twice. That is significant because of what happened that made God so angry at Solomon:

> The LORD appeared to Solomon the second time, as He had appeared to him at Gibeon. And the LORD said to him: "I have heard your prayer and your supplication that you have made before Me; I have consecrated this house which you have built to put My name there forever, and My eyes and My heart will be there perpetually. Now if you walk before Me as your father David walked, in integrity of heart and in uprightness, to do according to all that I have commanded you, and if you keep My statutes and My judgments, then I will establish the throne of your kingdom over Israel forever (1 Kings 9:2-5).

In these verses, God is telling Solomon that He has blessed him—blessed his labor and blessed the temple he built—and that if Solomon would walk before God as David did, with integrity and uprightness, and if he would do all that God commanded and keep His statutes and judgments, then He would continue to bless Solomon. This is a very important reminder from God, because

He had now appeared to Solomon twice and was now angry. This time when God appeared to Solomon, He told him that if he would just do these things, he would receive blessings. And then comes the "but" flipside, where God adds this:

> But if you or your sons turn away from me and do not observe the commands and decrees I have given you and go off to serve other gods and worship them, then I will cut off Israel from the land I have given them and will reject this temple I have consecrated for my Name. Israel will then become a byword and an object of ridicule among all peoples (1 Kings 9:6-7, NIV).

God is telling Solomon that if he turns from God and His ways, He'll bring Solomon down, bring the nation down, and bring Solomon's name down. Why is that important? Because God had already told him once, and now He is repeating it. God got angry with Solomon not just because Solomon did what he did, but because God had warned Solomon and still Solomon chose to disobey what God had told him when He first appeared to Solomon in a dream at Gibeon:

> At Gibeon the LORD appeared to Solomon during the night in a dream, and God said, "Ask for whatever you want me to give to you." Solomon answered, "You have shown great kindness to your servant, my father David, because he was faithful to you and righteous and upright in heart. You have continued this great kindness to him and have given him a son to sit on his throne this very day. Now, O LORD my God, you have made your servant king in place of my father David. But I am only a little child and do not know how to carry out my duties" (1 Kings 3:5-7, NIV)

Solomon made his one simple request of God: "Give your servant a discerning heart to govern your people and to distinguish between right and wrong" (1 Kings 3:9, NIV). Solomon asked for a discerning heart, for wisdom, and for just enough insight to lead God's people. So, being pleased with Solomon's request, God responded accordingly:

> Because you have asked this thing, and have not asked long life for yourself, nor have asked riches for yourself, nor have asked the life of your enemies, but have asked for yourself understanding to discern justice, behold, I have done according to your words; see, I have given you a wise and understanding heart, so that there has not been anyone like you before you, nor shall any like you arise after you. And I have also given you what you have not asked: both riches and honor, so that there shall not be anyone like you among the kings all your days. So if you walk in My ways, to keep My statutes and My commandments, as your father David walked, then I will lengthen your days (1 Kings 3:11-14).

Solomon never asked God for a dime; he only asked for wisdom, for judgment and discernment in leading God's people. God was so pleased that Solomon had asked for nothing for himself that God not only gave him the wisdom he requested, but He also gave him a blank check and made him the richest person who had ever lived. Here's the point: in 1 Kings 9:3-5, God was emphasizing how He had blessed Solomon, He had answered Solomon's prayer, and He had given him riches and honor—for which Solomon didn't even ask.

When was the last time God gave you a blank check? Have you ever received a blessing for something you didn't ask for? Have there been times in your life when the favor of God on you was so great that He not only gave you what you asked for, but He gave you things you didn't ask for—not because you were so good, but it was just the favor and grace of God? God wanted Solomon to realize how much He had blessed him. In the same way, God wants you to know that you may not think He has blessed you the way you think you ought to have been blessed, but if you look around, you will realize some visible, tangible evidence of His grace, mercy, longsuffering, provision and love for you. God wants us to get the message that He was giving to Solomon: *I have blessed you in spite of what you may think.* He blesses us in spite of us.

But now it gets sticky. The first time God appeared to Solomon, He told him He was going to bless him. The second time God appeared, He warned Solomon not to mess up, and that if he did, he would pay for it. Now let's move ahead in the story, to chapter 11 of 1 Kings, to discover what it was that Solomon did to make God so mad: "The LORD became angry with Solomon because his heart had turned away from the LORD, the God of Israel" (v. 9, *NIV*). The fact that Solomon had turned his heart away from God was only the half of it. *How* Solomon's heart turned was the key to God's anger: "King Solomon loved many foreign women" (1 Kings 11:1). The *King James Version* puts it like this: "King Solomon loved many strange women."

First Kings 11:3 reveals the extent of Solomon's indulgence: he had 700 wives, plus 300 concubines on the side. But the hook is in verse 2, where God reiterates to Solomon what He had already told Israel about all these women: "You must not intermarry with them, because they will surely turn your hearts after other gods." Which means don't go spend the night at their house and don't let them come spend the night at your house, don't intermarry with them, don't play house with them, don't date them, don't have sexual relations with them. But Solomon had ignored that admonition and cleaved to, grabbed hold of and hotly pursued *hundreds* of women from other countries, clans and beliefs, including Moabites, Ammonites, Edomites, Sidonians and Hittites.

God had warned Solomon that these women would turn his heart away from Him. And that's exactly what happened. God became angry because Solomon disobeyed Him and because his heart was turned. The hook was the warning. *Stay away from those women because they will turn your heart to other gods and idols.*

The lesson is that God gets angry when you love anything that will make you risk your love for Him. The implication of the text is that Solomon loved these women. But Solomon was supposed to love God first and foremost, and that meant to obey what God had told him to do and not to do. It was out of God's love for Solomon that He warned him. *If you love Me enough, obey Me.*

Anger is related to God's holiness; and His holiness responds to all sin and disobedience, because they go against His very nature. When you engage in sin, before you know it you will stop praying, you will stop reading, you will stop worshipping, you will stop submitting, you will stop trusting, you will stop sacrificing, and you'll be out in the woods somewhere, way off course. God's anger against Solomon was because he had allowed his heart to be turned away from Him. Solomon's excuse was that he was in love. He justified each of his hundreds of relationships with, "But I love her."

## Punishment Will Come

Is there someone in your life whom you hold on to so tightly that you are willing to risk your entire relationship with God? Does that person enhance or inhibit your walk with God? Here's the catch: we assume that because God didn't do anything, He's probably not going to do anything. But what the story of Solomon and his wives revealed is that there is a timeline with God. In Psalm 50:17-21, the sins the people were committing were against God's will. In Psalm 50:21, God responded, "These things you have done and I kept silent; you thought I was altogether like you. But I will rebuke you and accuse you to your face (*NIV*)." The people thought that because they had gotten away with it and God didn't do or say anything about it then, that He must be like them, which means that if God didn't do or say anything, everything must be okay. God' must not have been all that upset. But the Bible says, again and again, that God is *slow to anger*; it doesn't say He won't get angry.

The prophecy of Micah is a fascinating revelation of the nature of God's anger. It is so providential (and almost weird) that I am proofreading this manuscript on the same day that my devotional reading is in the book of Micah. Through this prophet, the Lord rebukes His people for their disobedience and "affairs" with other gods. Micah says that God has had enough. He condemns the preachers and prophets who lead His people astray. Yet, he predicts the return of God's people to Jerusalem to a restored Temple and the expectation of a time of peace. He prophesies the coming Messiah out of Bethlehem and reminds them that He loved them enough to redeem them. "I delivered you from a bad life in Egypt; I paid a good price to get you out of slavery" (Mic. 6:4, *THE MESSAGE*). He uses the picture of his contemporary, Hosea, by dramatizing his love in the image of Hosea and Gomer. The prophecy ends with Micah describing God in a powerful view into the nature of God:

> Where is the god who can compare with you—wiping the slate clean of guilt, turning a blind eye, a deaf ear, to the past sins of your purged and precious people? You don't nurse your anger and don't stay angry long, for mercy is your specialty. That's what you love most. And compassion is on its way to us. You stamp out our wrongdoing. You'll sink our sins to the bottom of the ocean (Mic. 7:18-19, *THE MESSAGE*).

We will examine more about the relationship between God's compassion, mercy, anger and love, but notice here that God gets angry—but slowly. When He does get angry, He doesn't fester in it and nurse it and milk it and linger in it. He doesn't stay angry long. I love that! Mixed in with His anger is compassion and mercy and love. What a mighty God we serve!

When you were growing up, did your mom or dad ever promise you a spanking? My mother used to promise us spankings. We'd do something wrong and Momma would say, "Alright. Alright," and she'd let us slide. Next time we did something, she'd say again, "Alright. Alright." What we were thinking was that she was forgetting about all the stuff we'd done. But somewhere down the road, Momma didn't have but one raw nerve left and the next time you did something, you hit it. "Go to the bathroom and wait for me," she would order us sternly. I used to wonder why Momma would send us to the bathroom. Then I realized that the bathroom was a cooling off period for Momma. That always tripped me up, because when she finally arrived, she would still spank me like crazy. I thought she must have not cooled off enough, but she was simply following Psalm 6:1: "Do not rebuke me in Your anger, nor chasten me in Your hot displeasure." Ebonics contemporary translation: "Lord, Momma, don't whup me while you're mad at me!" Her waiting was actually love, because by not reacting in the moment of her anger, Momma was saying, "Boy, if I hit you now, it'll be really bad!"

Momma had instant recall memory, too. She used to spank me for stuff I'd forgotten I had done that she'd let slide. All my disobedience had piled up and she said, *Enough!* The question for you to ask yourself is, *How many times has God let me slide?* How many times have you thought you got something past God? There's a funny, cute little movie called *Four Christmases*. In the movie, there's a scene where the lead female character tells her boyfriend, "I took a pregnancy test." The boyfriend assumes that meant she was pregnant, and he freaks out. So she tells him, "No, it was negative. But it did make me think about our relationship." How many times has God warned you and let you slide? How many scares have you had?

The manifestation of God's anger demonstrates the priority of purity, the seriousness of sin and the obligation of obedience.

We will learn about how God responds to His anger in a later chapter, but for now, I want you to ask God a very dangerous question: "Lord, are you mad at me?" What might God be mad at you for? First, He might be angry if you've been complaining. Second, He might be angry if you've allowed something into your life that hinders you from fulfilling all that He has called you to be and do. And third, God might be angry with you if He has warned you over and over again, yet you keep doing it over and over again.

Ask God to speak to your heart, to cleanse you—your mind and your spirit. Ask Him to bind the complaining spirit, bind the hindering spirit, bind the disobedient spirit. Ask Him to draw you closer to Him so that you might bring glory to Him. Ask Him to search your heart and your mind; and if there is anything in your life that stands between you and Him, ask Him and He will give you the power to say *no!*

God does not want to be angry at you. He wants to take great pride and joy in you, for, as Psalm 30:5 promises, "His anger lasts only a moment, but his favor lasts a lifetime; weeping may remain for a night, but rejoicing comes in the morning" (*NIV*).

*You are a forgiving God, gracious and compassionate,*
*slow to anger and abounding in love.*
NEHEMIAH 9:17, *NIV*

## REFLECTION QUESTIONS

1. Do you think it's possible that God could become so angry with you that He might not even speak to you? If not, why do you believe this way?

2. If you do believe it is possible for God to become so angry that He won't speak to you, why do you feel this way? What is one instance in your life where you have felt this to be the case?

3. What is the definition of "theodicy"?

4. If the source of God's jealousy is the result of a violation of *what God owns*, then what is God's anger the result of?

5. What might God be angry at you for right now? What will you do about that?

6. What are three examples of what makes God angry?

# 4

# The God Who Suffers

*My God, My God, why have You forsaken Me? Why are You
so far from helping Me, and from the words of My groaning? O My God,
I cry in the daytime, but You do not hear; and in the night season, and am
not silent. But You are holy, enthroned in the praises of Israel. Our fathers
trusted in You; they trusted, and You delivered them. They cried to You,
and were delivered; they trusted in You, and were not ashamed. But I am
a worm, and no man; a reproach of men, and despised by the people.
All those who see Me ridicule Me; they shoot out the lip, they shake the
head, saying, "He trusted in the LORD, let Him rescue Him; let Him
deliver Him, since He delights in Him!"*

PSALM 22:1-8

There are a wide variety of emotions displayed in the book of the
Psalms. It doesn't matter what state of mind you're in, there's a psalm
that will draw you into the presence and passion of God. And there's
a psalm that will match every emotion in the human experience.

Have you ever been in church while you're going through in-
credible difficulty in your life, and the pastor tells the congregation, "Everyone turn to the person beside you and tell them *good
morning!*" And your jaw clenches and you think, *I don't want to look
at nobody. I don't want to talk to anyone. Don't lay a hand on me. Don't
high five me, low five me or no five me, because I'm going through some stuff
right now and I'm struggling here!* You know—those days when you go
to church but you really don't feel like being there, don't feel like
raising your hands, don't want to turn to anyone, don't have a smile
to send out to your face. In fact, you did good just to be there.
Sometimes our greatest testimony is, "I'm here, God. I ain't got

much, I ain't brought much, but I'm here. I made it." When you're suffering a lot, you don't always want to share with others.

Does God ever suffer like we do? When we read Scripture, it's often through our own perspective, from the sinner's viewpoint, the wounded person's point of view. But as we examine the trials and struggles that we all face now and then, we're going to study a topic from a different perspective: the perspective of a God who knows how we feel when we are suffering, because He has suffered at least as much—and probably much more. But here's the difference: we suffer when we sin, but God suffers because we sin.

In the movie *The Godfather,* a character named Michael Corleone (portrayed by the actor Al Pacino) first appears as a young hero returning from World War II, destined to take over the family business, a New York organized crime syndicate.[1] By the third installment of the story, Michael has lived a life of crime and ungodliness, interspersed with a few charitable motives, with high and lofty values of family, and with some loyalty sprinkled here and there. By the time several generations of the fictional Sicilian Corleone family has been portrayed during the movie and its two sequels, Michael's life has degenerated to a climax of a silent cry of sorrow, pain and suffering so deep and so profound that it simply cannot be voiced. His suffering and anguish come at the apex of the life of this man who has touched the lives of many, was feared by many, and was loved by many.

Interestingly, the drama of this character's life is metaphorically depicted in a climactic scene during an opera. The opera is a tragedy that foretells another tragedy that will viciously thrust itself into Michael Corleone's life, leaving him forever changed. But the depth of his suffering and sorrow, captured in this violent moment in *The Godfather III,* highlights the kind of sorrow that, on one level or another during our lives, we all experience. It's a level of suffering that causes such a deep pain that we are void of the ability to express it; and in the pain of our sorrow, all we can do is silently cry out.

In this scene, Corleone's only daughter is gunned down in the crowded opera house by a man who meant to shoot Corleone himself—but his daughter inadvertently moves into the bullet's path.

As she lays dying in his arms, Corleone clings tightly to her, seemingly in an attempt to absorb her pain, to make it end, to bring it into himself and save her ebbing life. And now this man who has lived such a horrifically ungodly life cries out to God. "Oh, God! Oh, God, no, *no!*" And this sorrow and suffering that he takes on—literally absorbing the anguish of his dying teenage daughter—produces within him an inexpressible cry of silent anguish.

## Inexpressible Sorrow and Pain

The Koreans have a word for the inexpressible frustration of sorrow and pain. They call it *"han."* *Han* is a depth of hopelessness and helplessness that renders expression impossible. You can't put it into words. It's a depth of suffering and sorrow that, at best, produces a painful, yet silent, cry out to God. You reach out and call to Him because you face a set of circumstances that you cannot fix, you cannot solve, you cannot even understand. This inexpressible pain sometimes moves to aggression. Sometimes it moves to passivity. Sometimes to resentment. It's a depth of suffering that is most characterized by intense loneliness, in the midst of which something in you cries out to our Maker.

That's where David was when he penned to God the words of the sad song of desperation that we know as Psalm 22. One of the things I like about songs is that they express our feelings when we are often left without words to express them. Songs give us verbiage, phrases and words that enable us to describe the indescribable. Thus, David cries out to God in Psalm 22, when he says, "My God, my God, why have You forsaken me?" Why are You so far from helping me, God? Why are You so far from the words of my roaring? I'm crying out, I'm calling to You. You're so far away I can't even hear You. "Forsaken" implies leaving someone in circumstances of tragedy and trial. Why have you left me like this? I cry out to You in the daytime and You don't even hear me. I call again at nighttime and You still don't hear me. Most of us immediately recognize in that phrase the same forsaken suffering spoken of by Jesus as He hung on the cross at Calvary: "My God, my God, why have You forsaken me?"

When we hear that phrase during Easter, we think of the cry of
Jesus from Matthew 27:46 and Mark 15:34. We hear it and examine
it from the standpoint of Jesus, and we put ourselves in His spot
and we remember those times when we too have called out that way.
*Lord, where are You? Where have You been? Why did You leave me?* We
can relate to His cry because we look at it from the perspective of
the crier, Jesus. But remember, He's saying *"My* God"—He's calling
out to God. Do you ever think about what God might have thought
when He heard His only Son crying out to Him and feeling abandoned by Him? It's one thing to hear it as the Son calling out to
the Father on Calvary, or David calling out to God; but try to imagine what God the Father must have felt like when the cries of His
Son indicated that His Son felt abandoned.

If you are a parent, when your child cries out to you when they
feel physical or emotional pain, you want to be there for them, you
want them to know that you hear them. You hear their cries *and* you
want to assure them that you hear them. There's a dual dimension to
cries of despair. One of the saddest memories I have of my mother
was the day I went to St. Louis to move her to Los Angeles. She had to
move out of the home she had lived in for 40 years (as long as I had
lived, at that point). The moving men were there, packing up all of
her things, and my mother sat down on the steps and cried like a baby.

"Son," she wept, "why are you doing this to me? Don't do this,
son. Why are you mad at me?"

"Momma," I told her, "the doctor told us you can't live by yourself any longer. You and your sister must make a decision."

Momma sat on those steps and cried her heart out. I heard her
cries, but imagine what was going through my mind as I was trying
to make a decision that was best for her while she was crying out to
me, "Why are you doing this?"

That was the situation on Calvary when Jesus said, *Father why
are you doing this to Me? Why are you allowing this to happen to Me?* Now
try to imagine what God must have felt like as His Son was crying
out to Him.

My momma begged me, "Son, don't do this to me. *Please* don't
do this to me. What did I do to you?"

She was pleading with me, crying out to me, as she was being taken from her home of decades. Yet, I was trying to act as a responsible son. It cut my heart. Now try to imagine what God the Father must have felt watching as His only begotten Son is hanged, suspended between earth and heaven, bloody on a cross, crying out, *Father! You've left me. You've forgotten me. You've forsaken me.* This was the same Jesus who, in John 10:30, said, "I and my Father are one"; and in John 14:9 said, "He who has seen Me has seen the Father." So, if Jesus was hanging on the cross and He cried out to the Father (with whom He is "one"), then it's not so much that God had abandoned Him, but that God was (inseparably) *with* Him. Yet, clouded by the darkness of Calvary, the human side of Jesus couldn't even recognize the Presence and the companionship of the very Father with whom Jesus said He is "one." He felt so alone that He felt divided within Himself and divided from Himself—His God self. Remember, it was not just Jesus on that cross, it was, as theologian Jürgen Moltmann put it, a crucified God on the cross.

So, it was not that God had abandoned Jesus. It was that He was experiencing the divine *han*, the hopelessness and helplessness of His humanity, blinded to the reality of the presence of God His Father. So He cried out, "Why have You forsaken me?"—when, in fact, He was crying out to Him Who was always "with" Him (for God never left Jesus, because God could never leave Himself). It's a conundrum that exists in the rift between reality and human feelings.

The life we live can throw stuff at us and blind us, confuse us and mess up our minds so much that we lose contact with truth, because reality of truth is overshadowed by the human struggle with pain and emotion in the suffering moment. We see here not only a Jesus who is suffering, but a God who is suffering. It's like when my mother suffered on those steps all those years ago and cried out to me. It cut my heart; there were two people suffering on those steps.

When Jesus hung on the cross, there were two Divine Beings suffering. Thus, it is clear that God is a God who can suffer. That almost sounds blasphemous. In fact, back in medieval times, that proposition was considered sacrilege. There was a period when there was the sense of God who was, in His very essence, immutable and impassable, meaning that God cannot change, that He cannot feel. However, the foundation of that premise is laid upon words such as "impassive," a negative form of the word "passion," which would indicate that God is impassionate and void of feeling. It paints a picture of a distant, transcendent God who is akin to, as some have described Him, a watchmaker creator who created heaven and earth and then wound it up and left it to tick away all on its own. Our God is not that way. A distant, disengaged, unconcerned, unmoved, unfeeling, uncaring God is not the God I know. I'd have a hard time worshiping a Lord like that.

Fortunately, Scripture indicates that premise to be false. God can relate to us in every way—our emotions, passions and all—because we were made in His image. And we are rife with passion. But it goes deeper than that. At the core of suffering is God's decision about unconditional love and the myriad emotional consequences thereof.

## True Love: An Invitation to Suffer?

There are three immutable characteristics and dimensions of God: God is light, God is holy, God is love. He *is* all three of these. As we learned in the first chapter, God does not simply love, He actually *is* love. In fact, God is love so much that He does not stop loving you depending on what you do and how you respond to His love; He loves you because He *is* eternal, endless, permanent love. Therefore, there is nothing that you can do to make God love you more, and there's nothing you can do to make God love you less.

However, there are different dimensions and manifestations of God's love. For, when you love someone, you give them the ability to hurt you. Because we only truly, deeply hurt the ones we love, and we are only truly, deeply, hurt by the ones we love. The gamble God took when He created us is that He loves us so much that He gave us a free will. And that free will includes the choice to love Him or not to love Him; to reject Him or to embrace Him. He made His choice; now the reciprocal choice is up to us.

Remember, John 1:11 tells us that God came unto His own and His own received Him not—the Jewish nation to whom He came chose to reject Him as the Messiah He is. But He loved them enough to allow them to choose not to love Him. And that's where reality can really hurt: When those He loves reject Him, turn from Him and disobey Him, it still hurts Him. He suffers from the pain inflicted by those He loves.

Sure, God is the Almighty. Yet, He has enough power to make Himself vulnerable, to put Himself in a position to get Himself rejected by those He loves. He offers Himself to us because He loves us. But He is so sensitive in His love for us that He hurts and is pained if we reject Him. He doesn't stop being God; He's just hurt by our rejection of His love, because—and this is important to grasp and accept—God was once human too. God walked the earth as the man Jesus, thereby subjecting Himself to everything humans can do to each other—and He felt every one of the emotions attached to the humanity He took upon Himself.

Thus, we do not have a God who cannot be touched with our weaknesses (see Heb. 4:15), because God understands what it's like when you are brokenhearted, because He too has had His heart broken. He understands what it's like when you've been betrayed, because He too has been betrayed. He knows what you're feeling when you've been rejected, because He too has felt the sting of those times when you rejected Him.

How does God suffer? What does the suffering of God look like? Let's count just a few of the ways.

## 1. God Suffers in Our Suffering

In Isaiah 63:9, the prophet says, "In all their affliction He was afflicted." The *New International Version* states the verse as, "In all their distress he too was distressed." God sees His children struggling and afflicted, and in all they are going through and feeling, He too is going through and feeling. With all of the trouble the people are going through, He is in their trouble with them. The *New International Version* uses the word "distress." God was distressed with them. The words "afflicted" and "affliction" mean "a narrow place." It's the metaphor for pain, struggle and oppression, of being hemmed in by the enemy, of having your back against the wall. When you're in that situation, you're in affliction.

I used to see that picture as us being in a tight place and God being on the outside, making room for us. That's what I see in Psalm 46:1. The same word for "trouble" or "affliction" is used there. However, in its context, God is revealed as the one we run to; the place of refuge we run to when we are in trouble. It is a spiritual "run" because we are "in trouble." The word implies a tight, narrow place.

That blesses me, but that's not the picture in Isaiah 63. This picture is of God stepping into the tightness of your situation, into the narrowness of your space, and suffering and struggling and straining right along with you. He does not leave you there to make your way and fight your way out by yourself, while He stands on the sidelines cheering you on. He is suffering *with* you. He steps into it with you because He loves you enough not to leave you there all by yourself. Thus, in your affliction, He is likewise afflicted. In all of your tight places and your small, hemmed-in spaces, as small as they are, they're still big enough for two occupants: you and the One who is there with you. So whatever you are going through right now in your life, move over, because God says that in all of your struggles, He's struggling right alongside you. In all of your pain, He's there with you. In your hurt, He's hurting too.

Isaiah 63:9 goes on to say, "In His love and in His pity He redeemed them; and He bore them and carried them." He doesn't just step in to offer you a shoulder to cry on. He doesn't join you in a private pity party. Out of His love, He chooses to step in with you and go through the suffering right with you. He comes in to take you through. And *through* means He may have come in through one side with you to pick you up and carry you out, if that's what it takes to bring you out of the mess. (Then He'll take all the glory, all the praise and all the credit, because that's what's due Him.)

I don't care what you're going through. I don't care how dark it is. I don't care how painful it is. The promise of God to you is that He has not left you nor forsaken you. He is deep in it right there with you.

## 2. God Suffers When We Betray Him

The Bible often uses a rhetorical device called a simile or a metaphor in expressing something that may be hard to fully understand. It's what you use when you're trying to explain the inexplicable to help someone really get it. For example, in Isaiah 42:14, God says, "I have held My peace a long time, I have been still and restrained Myself. Now I will cry like a woman in labor, I will pant and gasp at once." In this verse, God uses something we're familiar with to show us what the unfamiliar thing is like. Another example might be when someone asks, "What is it like to want for God?" the answer is that it's like being a deer that pants for water (see Ps. 42:1). That's a simile.

God uses this striking simile in Isaiah 42:14 to describe His suffering over the disobedience of the Israelites, who have hurt Him so much that He cries out, telling them that He is suffering like a woman going through labor pains. He gasps and pants at the same time, which means He has to check His breathing, because He's so cut on the inside that the pain is like a woman having a baby. If you've ever been through childbirth, then you understand in an instant the pain to which God is referring. Until you have borne a child of your own, you can't even begin to imagine what that pain is like.

That's physical pain. But there is pain that is equal to that: Emotional pain. God wanted us to know, through one particular prophet, what emotional pain, suffering and rejection felt like to Him, so He came up with a very unique way to show us how He suffers:

> When the LORD began to speak through Hosea, the LORD said to him, "Go, take to yourself an adulterous wife and children of unfaithfulness, because the land is guilty of the vilest adultery in departing from the LORD." So he married Gomer daughter of Diblaim, and she conceived and bore him a son. . . . The LORD said to me, "Go, show your love to your wife again, though she is loved by another and is an adulteress. Love her as the LORD loves the Israelites, though they turn to other gods and love the sacred raisin cakes." So I bought her for fifteen shekels of silver and about a

homer and a lethek of barley. Then I told her, "You are to live with me many days; you must not be a prostitute or be intimate with any man, and I will live with you" (Hos. 1:2-3; 3:1-3, *NIV*).

God also suffers like a betrayed lover. When Hosea tells God he's ready to prophesy to the people, God tells him he's not really ready yet, because he doesn't understand how deeply God loves Israel and how the Israelites treat Him. Before God will release Hosea to speak for Him, He wants the prophet to learn how to feel like God feels.

God tells Hosea that there's a prostitute named Gomer and that Hosea is to go and marry Gomer and love her with the same love God loves Israel. So, Hosea marries the whore named Gomer. And what kind of first lady does Gomer make, behaving the way she does? True to her nature, she cheats on Hosea, sneaks out in the middle of the night, hops from bed to bed to bed with different guys. She even gets pregnant by other men. Then she becomes a slave and is pimped out, put on the auction block and sold like a common streetwalker.

God then tells Hosea to go and buy her back—Hosea, the man of God, the prophet! Go down to the public auction block, bid on Gomer and buy her back. Hosea tells God he can't do that. God tells him he will do it, because only then will the prophet understand how God feels when Israel cheats on Him and whores around behind His back. So Hosea goes down as a bruised and betrayed lover and suffers the humiliation of walking through the section of the little village where they charge by the half hour and people are wagging their fingers and whispering to each other as he strides past them, saying, "Here comes the prophet, husband of the prostitute." And he walks boldly down to the auction block and gives them enough to redeem her, the price to buy her out of the slavery into which she had chosen to put herself.

This is a picture of a God who suffers when He has been betrayed. He suffers when He has been denied, when we cheat and commit adultery on Him. Yet He loves us so much that He sends

His Son Jesus to stand on the auction block of Calvary and He bids with His nailed hands and feet. He bids with a crown of thorns crushed into His head. He bids with a spear thrust into His side. He bids with His very life. *I will buy back this ungodly man. I will redeem him of My own spirit.*

God suffers like a betrayed lover.

## 3. God Suffers Like a Broken Father

In Luke 15:11-13, Jesus tells the story of a lost son:

> There was a man who had two sons. The younger one said to his father, "Father, give me my share of the estate." So he divided his property between them. Not long after that, the younger son got together all he had, set off for a distant country and there squandered his wealth in wild living (*NIV*).

It's interesting that Jesus never calls the younger son a *prodigal* son. That's because the word "prodigal" means "extravagant," "generous" and "costly." Thus, the truth of the story is not about a prodigal son but a prodigal father, because it is the father whose love is so extravagant, so costly and so generous that when his son looks him in the eyes and demands his share of the inheritance, the father gives it to him without argument.

He is a man of wisdom who knows what the angry world holds in store for his son. Yet, he lets him go. Nowhere in that text does it say that the father tries to talk him out of it. Nowhere in the text does he try to hold on to a child who is bent on having his own way. The father simply loves him enough to let him go, rather than cling to him or force him to stay.

It's like the story of the little boy who had a pet canary that he loved dearly. Every day in school he would think about his favorite pet. He would come home from school and cuddle and pet that little canary. One day, the boy came home and discovered that the canary had gotten out of the cage and was lost. When they found it, the little boy was overjoyed, hugging and caressing that little canary, telling it how much he missed it, and hugging and squeezing and caressing

it until he opened his hand . . . and discovered the little bird had suf-
focated to death. The boy's love choked the life out of his beloved
little pet. Sometimes you've got to love enough to let them go.

The son wasted his inheritance on riotous, wild living—parties,
wine and women—until he lost everything he'd been given. All of
the scenes in the story are of the rebellious son. But flip the script
and you'll see how God suffers: He suffers like a parent whose child
is wayward. Like a parent who doesn't even know where that son or
daughter is. God suffers like a parent who has done everything possible to provide for a child who is ungrateful and unthankful and
walked out. God suffers like a father who looks out the window
every day, hoping to see his child coming down the lane. Like a father who looks at the phone every day to see if there's a voicemail.
He suffers like a parent who has no idea what happened to His
child. Has he died? Is she alive? Has he been killed? Is he broke? Is
she sleeping on someone's floor? Where is my child? God suffers
like a parent broken by the betrayal of an ungrateful child, but held
together by a love that refuses to quit.

God suffers like the prodigal father who looks and looks and
looks, until one day, down the dusty road, he sees the familiar gait
of a figure off in the distance, slowly plodding along, head down,
shoulders slumped. And this dignified Jewish father picks up his
robes and does what no dignified Jew would do—he runs to his
child! He won't wait until the child walks up to him and falls on
his face in apology. He runs to get his wayward, returning child!
That's how God is. He suffers when we betray Him—yet He is always
watching for us, endlessly hoping we will come home to Him.

> And it was right and proper that God, who made everything
> for his own glory, should allow Jesus to suffer, for in doing
> this he was bringing vast multitudes of God's people to
> heaven; for his suffering made Jesus a perfect Leader, one
> fit to bring them into their salvation. . . . For since he him-
> self has now been through suffering and temptation, he
> knows what it is like when we suffer and are tempted, and
> he is wonderfully able to help us (Heb. 2:10,18, *TLB*).

Kenneth C. Ulmer

# A Suffering God Who Loves Us Permanently

Hebrews 5:8 states that although Jesus "was a Son, he learned obedience through what he suffered" (*NRSV*). We serve a God who suffers with us. It does not matter what you are going through today, you serve a God who steps into your sorrow. He's the same God who stepped into Calvary not just to hang in disgrace on that cross, but to come off that cross and go into a tomb long enough to let His enemies think they had won. But early the following Sunday morning, He walked out of that tomb with all power and heaven and earth in His hands and then gave us that same power. You have the power to make it through your Calvary of sorrow and be resurrected in victory; the power to come out on the other side of what seemed to be a victory for the enemy.

In Psalm 3:1-2, David writes, "O LORD, so many are against me. So many seek to harm me. I have so many enemies. So many say that God will never help me" (*TLB*). These verses describe the circumstances of David's suffering when he was forced to flee from his son Absalom, who was trying to dethrone his own father. *Lord, there are so many who surround me. Many there are who mock me saying where is your God?*

You may have some people like that in your life right now. You might be going through some trying challenges, and folks who know that you go to church every Sunday are wondering, *Well, if you go to church every Sunday, then why are you suffering the hell you're going through?* But the psalmist adds, in the next verse, "But Lord, you are my shield, my glory, and my only hope. You alone can lift my head, now bowed in shame" (Ps. 3:3, *TLB*). That's the God we serve. That's the God who invites us to come on back home. That's the God who says to you today, *This is your day to say yes.* The God who tells you that, in spite of what you're been through, you're still here, and what is coming is better than what has been. The God who sent His Son to redeem and reclaim you, and if you would but say yes to Him on this day, then He would become your Lord and Savior even through your suffering. The God who knows our suffering because He has suffered over us, is the same God who brought you to today so He could let you know that what you're going through, you are not going through all alone. Psalm 3:3 says, "But You, O LORD, are a shield for me. My glory and the One who lifts up my head." Whatever you're experiencing, God is your shield.

In the Greek army, there were two kinds of shields: the shield you wore on your arm for battle, and the long shield, which was wide and tall enough for you to crouch behind so it would protect you from the attacks and arrows of the enemy. God is the long shield God, the God who surrounds you and protects you when the enemy is trying to take you out.

The best thing about our God who suffers when we desert Him, cheat on Him, disobey Him, is that He *never* walks out on us. What a mighty God we serve!

*If you love, you will suffer, and if you do not love,*
*you do not know the meaning of a Christian life.*
AGATHA CHRISTIE (1890-1976)

## REFLECTION QUESTIONS

1. When was a time you felt forsaken by friends or family, or maybe even by God Himself?

2. What was the outcome in that particular situation?

3. What are two ways in which God suffers?

4. Why does God suffer when we desert Him or disobey Him?

5. Where is God when you are suffering?

**Note**
1. The Francis Ford Coppola-directed movie based on the Mario Puzo novel *The Godfather*.

# The God Who Grieves

*The LORD saw how great man's wickedness on the earth had become,*
*and that every inclination of the thoughts of his heart was only evil*
*all the time. The LORD was grieved that he had made man on the earth,*
*and his heart was filled with pain. So the LORD said, "I will wipe man-*
*kind, whom I have created, from the face of the earth—men and animals,*
*and creatures that move along the ground, and birds of the air—*
*for I am grieved that I have made them."*
GENESIS 6:5-7, *NIV*

Can God become so grieved, so distressed, so anguished that He changes His mind? Genesis 6:6 introduces an attribute of God that is often a source of much debate. To say that God "changed His mind" seems to be a glaring counterpoint to the doctrines of *immutability* and *impassibility*. While these two attributes are not identical, they are related: the former suggests that God does not change, while the latter refers to the impossibility of God being acted upon by an outside influence. Often (but not always), immutability has been interpreted as meaning that God cannot be "moved" in an emotional sense. However, Genesis 6:5-7 paints a powerful picture of a grieving God with a broken heart.

One of my favorite movies is *Something the Lord Made*. It is the story of Dr. Alfred Blalock, an arrogant cardiologist, and Vivien Thomas, his African-American assistant who had no college training. Together, they invent bypass surgery during the realities of Depression Era racism. In one scene, the doctors are performing an operation in an operating theater where other physicians are observing the procedure. The audience can hear everything being said by the surgeons. Imagine hearing one of those doctors saying "Oops" during surgery. That's the last thing you ever want to hear a surgeon say while he's working.

Now imagine God saying, "*Oops*—didn't mean that." It's hard to imagine God making a mistake or changing His mind. Words like "repent," "relent" and "change" don't quite fit into the personhood of omnipotence. That's why I am intellectually and theologically puzzled by passages like the following ones:

> God then sent the angel to Jerusalem but when he saw the destruction about to begin, he compassionately *changed his mind* and ordered the death angel, "Enough's enough! Pull back!" (1 Chron. 21:15, *THE MESSAGE,* emphasis added).

> And God *did think twice*. He decided not to do the evil he had threatened against his people (Exod. 32:14, *THE MESSAGE,* emphasis added).

One of the first things we notice when we examine texts like these is that the various translations and interpretations of these words say that God "repented" or "changed His mind" or "did think twice" are all synonymous with attempts to transport a description of one of the passions of God into language we mere mortals can understand.

## Seeing God from Man's Point of View

The first mention of the idea of God changing his mind is found in Genesis 6:5-7, which paints a powerful picture of a grieving God with a broken heart. In Genesis 6, God sees the drastic disparity between how He created man and what man has become. God's "divine grief" is a passionate portrait of His painful disappointment in the creation He loves, because man has degenerated from the image of God in which he was made and has become skilled in choosing the wrong ways, making bad decisions and taking paths of evil instead of good. Man consistently steps over boundaries set by God and continually violates His principles and laws. The core of man's being has become corrupt, and his actions, aspirations and attitudes are antithetical to the character of his Creator.

It grieves God that man has made a conscious determination to go contrary to His ways. In short, *man has a heart problem*; and that fills God's heart with pain, because He loves us so much. This love of God for man is hurting Him so bad that it appears that God changed His mind and wishes He had not even created man. However, in actuality, the focus and emphasis of these passages is on the pain of God more than on the change of God.

Arthur Pink helps us grapple with this unchanging God who "changed his mind," by lifting other metaphors of God that do not contradict, but compliment the idea of a mind-changing God. Pink exegetes the Genesis 6 passage as one of the frequent occasions when God accommodates His language to our limited capacities: He speaks in His divinity, but we hear in our humanity. Pink says that God, "speaks of Himself as 'waking' [Ps. 78:65], as 'rising early' [Jer. 7:13]; yet He neither slumbers nor sleeps."[1]

Deuteronomy 32:4 states that God is always the same. He is an immovable rock, the never-fluctuating Deity, unchangeable in His essence, His attributes and His counsel. James 1:17 tells us that God never changes or varies. In Exodus 3:14, He calls Himself "I AM." The great I AM is always *AM*, never *Was*, never *Will Be*. Contrary to the implications of so-called "process theology," God is not processing, He's not "becoming," He is not "evolving" into something He has never been. In God's desire to be known, it is as if He reveals Himself and speaks of Himself in *our* "language," switching places, taking our position as the hearer of what He is revealing about Himself, and using words, concepts and ideas as we humans would hear them.

In his book *The Doctrine of God*, Veli-Matti Kärkkäinen, professor of systemic theology at Fuller Seminary, wrote, "Clearly, the Bible never attempts to speak of God in Godself but rather in relation to humans."[2] God wants to be known, and therefore chooses to "reveal himself in a way that, at least to some extent, can be understood."[3]

The Genesis 6:6 description of God being grieved that He made man means the sinfulness of man displeased Him so much that, as seventeenth-century Baptist preacher Benjamin Keach wrote in *Preaching from the Types and Metaphors of the Bible,* "God manifested His divine decree to punish them. Repentance is ascribed to God, by which likewise his divine displeasure against men's iniquities, and the infliction of punishment is in line with the emotional character of God."[4]

It is important to note that God in grief is not God in anger. During the Great Awakening Revival of the 1740s, evangelist Jonathan Edwards shook a Connecticut town with a sermon filled with hellfire and brimstone. It was titled "Sinners in the Hands of an Angry God." Many people turned to the Lord during this powerful message of sin, hell and the wrath of an angry God. This may have been a powerful and appropriate message for the time (and I certainly don't intend to deny that the love of God is often demonstrated by His anger over ungodliness), but it is important to understand that the Genesis 6 passage and related passages about the God who is grieved, who repents, who changes His mind or who is sorry are *not* examples of an angry God, but of a God who grieves over what we do.

One of the challenges faced by the Church is the distorted image of an "angry God." This picture has been used to threaten people into the Kingdom (thus replacing freedom of choice with fear of vengeance). The angry God who is "out to get sinners" is utterly contrary to the God who so loved the world that He gave His only Son (see John 3:16). While Scripture does present divine judgment in the biblical story, this text is not such a depiction. This passage (and others like it) present us with the pathos of God, the pain of God, the anguish of God, in response to the ungodliness of humanity.

The broader view of the *judgment* of God must include the heart of God, which is broken over sin and must, eventually, do something to deal with it. The *grief* of God, on the other hand, goes deeper than the anger of God. We discover a ray of hope in the broken heart of God that even in His grief there is the glow of His great mercy.

# Seeing God From God's Point of View

A flag that is raised in the Genesis 6:6 scenario is the idea of God actually changing His mind about having made mankind. This idea is hard to get our minds around—until we understand that the translation to the English word repented is actually *not* the most accurate translation of the Hebrew word. The word translated as "repented" in the *King James Version* is best translated as grieved (as translated in the *New International Version*). Notice that the word is translated as "grieved" in the *New International Version*, repented in the *King James Version*, and as sorry in the *New King James Version, New Revised Standard Version, New American Standard Bible, New Century Version* and others. There is a slightly different connotation to the passage when you read, "it grieved God": put this way, the word does not suggest that God changed His mind. In fact the Bible seems to clearly and definitively say that God does *not* change His mind (see Mal. 3:6, 1 Sam. 15:29, Heb. 13:8, Jas. 1:17), but He does grieve over our sinful actions.

Humanity struggles to describe and relate to the idea of God repenting and changing His mind. Yet Genesis 6:6 says it "repented God" (*KJV*). In his book *The Nature and Character of God*, W. A. Pratney gives this interpretation of Genesis 6:6:

It seems clear that God was initially happy over His creation, and that the space-time fall of man and the subsequent spread of deep rebellion brought Him real grief. In Genesis 6:6-7 (and 37 other times in the Bible) the special word *nacham* is used for "repent." It comes from a root that means "to draw the breath forcibly, to pant, to breathe strongly, to groan," and is difficult to translate into English. It is usually used of God instead of the word *shuwb* used of man's repentance, his turning from sin. Zodiates writes, "Essentially *nacham* is a change of heart or disposition, a change of mind, purpose, or conduct. When a man changes his attitude, God makes the corresponding change. God is morally bound not to change His stance if man continues to travel on an evil path . . ." When God

did change His mind it was because of the intercession of
man and because of man's true repentance [Exodus 32:12-
14; Jeremiah 31:19-20; Jonah 3:10]. God is consistent
[Psalm, 110:4; James 1:17]. Though it may appear that
God's purpose has changed, according to God's perspective nothing has changed. Most prophecy is conditional
upon the response of man.[5]

In other words, our unchanging God loves us so much that
He gave man the option and ability to *not* love Him (for, how else
would He be able to have true relationship with us, as relationship
does result from one person forcing the other into such relationship). However, this unchanging God who does not change His
mind, does *respond* to the changeability and sinful nature of man.
To say (using the less accurately-translated word in the *King James
Version*) that "God repented" means that there was a change in *man*
to which God responded in a manner that was consistent with His
unchanging holiness, but was interpreted and perceived in the
mind of *man* as "a change of heart" (or what we would describe as
God "repenting").

Man must learn through theoscopic vision; that is, seeing
from God's perspective. God tells us in Isaiah 55:8-9 that no matter how close we get, even in our sincerest motives, there will always be a gap between His thoughts and ways, and ours. Once we
acknowledge and accept the tension of this spiritual reality, it is
easier to take the simple revelation of God changing His mind as
an example of God from our human perspective. Pratney quotes
British theologian/philosopher C. S. Lewis's classic work *The Problem of Pain* to shed light on this issue:

If God sometimes speaks as though the Impassible could
suffer passion and as if eternal fullness could be in want . . .
this can mean only, if it means anything intelligible by us,
that the God of mere miracle has made Himself able to
hunger and created in Himself that which we can satisfy.
If He requires us, the requirement is of His own choosing.

If the immutable heart can be grieved by the puppets of His own making, it is Divine omniscience that has so subjected it freely and in a humility that passes understanding. . . . If He who is Himself can lack nothing chooses to need us, it is because we need to be needed.[6]

In other words, the omnipotence of God includes the power and ability to limit His own omnipotence. God is powerful enough to selectively restrain His power. It is out of His eternal love that God allows us to disobey Him and to choose to walk contrary to His will. The flip side is that God's eternal love for us contains a self-imposed vulnerability to our disobedience—yet a vulnerability that *will* cause Him to respond to that disobedience within the framework and boundaries of His immutable, never-changing holiness. Any scenario that finds God changing is not arbitrary; it is always a change from our finite perspective, and it is always God changing in response to our change. When God says He will destroy Israel, for example, He changes His mind when Israel *"repents of its evil"* (see Jer. 18:7-10; emphasis added).

In the book of 2 Chronicles, a conversation between God and Solomon helps us understand the issue of a mind-changing God. Eugene Peterson's *THE MESSAGE* captures God's word to Solomon from 2 Chronicles 7:17-21:

As for you, if you live in my presence as your father David lived, pure in heart and action, living the life I've set out for you, attentively obedient to my guidance and judgments, then I'll back your kingly rule over Israel—make it a sure thing on a sure foundation. The same covenant guarantee I gave to David your father I'm giving to you, namely, "You can count on always having a descendant on Israel's throne." But if you or your sons betray me, ignoring my guidance and judgments, taking up with alien gods by serving and worshiping them, then the guarantee is off: I'll wipe Israel right off the map and repudiate this Temple I've just sanctified to honor my Name. And Israel will be nothing but a bad joke among the peoples of the world (*THE MESSAGE*).

At first, as 1 Kings 3:3 relates, "Solomon loved God and continued to live in the God-honoring ways of David his father, except that he also worshiped at the local shrines, offering sacrifices and burning incense" (*THE MESSAGE*). But as his career and fame as King of Israel spreads across the then-known world and Solomon becomes the wisest and wealthiest man in the world, he "openly defied GOD; he did not follow in his father David's footsteps. . . . Solomon faithlessly disobeyed GOD's orders" (1 Kings 11:6,10, *THE MESSAGE*). So, God keeps His word and pronounces judgment on Solomon and his kingdom. He doesn't destroy the entire nation, but He keeps His promise that if Solomon turns from the Lord, he will suffer at the hand of God.

God intended and desired to bless Solomon—and He did, as long as Solomon kept his word and walked in righteousness. But when Solomon decided to go off the path and walk in disobedience, it voided God's blessings and triggered His caveat of punishment for disobedience. You might say that God changed His mind; however, He had clearly laid down the terms of the agreement up front, and it obviously was His desire to bless Solomon. The impending judgment was the result of Solomon's sin—he chose to cancel the arrangement, and God's judgment then kicked in.

So, did God change His mind, or did He act in response to His holiness? It's clear that the so-called change of mind by God in Genesis 6:6 was actually His holy response of broken-heartedness over the pervasive sinfulness of His creation.

It is interesting that, although the translation "God repented" does not convey the accurate meaning of God's action in our contemporary understanding of the word "repent," when you look at that word in the language of the New Testament, "repent" actually means "to turn, or to change one's direction, to change the mind." It suggests a change of heart. And that is what God wants you to do when you sin. He wants you to repent and realize that what you did is not the will of God. Change your direction and return to

Him. Realize that there is a loving God who is waiting with open arms to receive, restore and renew the love He eternally has for you. His love is always open and waiting for our repentance.

## God's First Grieving... and the Wages Thereof

Man started a downhill journey away from the will and way of God when sin entered the Garden of Eden. By the time Genesis 6 came around, it was as if God said to Adam what He would one day say to Solomon: That's it! The blessings are off! I'm done—you're out of here. In His grief over the Fall, God was sorry that He made mankind.[7] And therein lies the lesson: Sin breaks the heart of God because His holiness is violated by our sin. Apostle Paul stated it this way: "The wages of sin is death" (Rom. 6:23). There is validity in saying that God repents (changes His mind) when *we don't* repent (refuse to change our mind about sin). It may sound like doubletalk, but it addresses the tension of the gap between His ways and thoughts, and our ways and thoughts.

Something always dies when we sin. In the case of man, in Genesis 6, man's sin led to judgment on the entire creation. Fortunately for us, the irrevocable attribute of God's holiness and love will always be the context in which judgment is dispensed. A parent disciplines a child out of love for the child. God disciplines His children out of His love for us (see Heb. 12:6). Even in discipline, the true parent never stops loving the child. We are fortunate that God loves us enough to discipline us, for only from discipline comes learning and growth.

God blesses because He loves. His loving intention and desire to bless is affected by our conscious decision to sin against His holiness. He is offended when His holiness is violated, and He responds in judgment—and knowingly risks being misunderstood by us as an uncaring, insensitive and harsh God, when in fact, it would violate God's own character were He not to respond in judgment. However (again, fortunately for us), that judgment is tempered, and even delayed, only by His own grace and mercy—which is the source of His forgiveness when we repent.

God's love is unconditional, but His ways toward man are *always* conditional. That is not a contradiction. For example, I love my children. There is nothing they could do to make me stop loving them. However, it is because of that very love that my "ways" toward them must be conditional. In other words, I love them too much to reward disobedience. I love them too much to allow waywardness to go unpunished. I love them too much to remain silent when I see them going the wrong way—especially when they do it with deliberate abandonment of the rules.

I have four children (three daughters and a son). They are all grown now, and my two oldest daughters have five daughters between them. When they were young, I often hesitated to speak or hand out discipline. I think this was due to my insecurity. I sometimes felt that if I punished them, denied them something or said "no," it might impact their love for me. But as much as it grieved me to see them disobey and to have to mete out appropriate recompense for their actions, I would always remind myself that I loved them, and it was that very love that compelled me to discipline them (thankfully, those times were rare).

Sometimes it meant cancellation of some "promise" to take them to an amusement park or buy them some treat or another toy (which they probably didn't need anyway). But did I change my mind? I'm sure it seemed that way to them. Did I change my love? Certainly not. And I definitely did not change my character (as a father). In fact, I reinforced and reemphasized my fatherhood by loving them enough to discipline them (whether they knew it at the time or not). Yet it grieved me when they disobeyed, and it grieved me when I had to dish out punishment. And so it is with God toward His children.

## What Will God Do?

Maybe the takeaway for us when we examine the God who grieves over our disobedience is that the tug and pull of our pondering becomes a real example of the same tension we experience when faced with betrayal, disobedience, temptation and sin. It's a good idea, before we plunge headlong into sin, to slow down long enough to stop and ask ourselves, "What will God do if I do this?" It is crucial that we ponder the consequences of our every decision to defy (and therefore displease and grieve) God. We can make the choice to sin, but we can't choose the consequences of our choice. Sin in our life short-circuits the power of God's blessings in our life. As much as He loves us, He loves us out of the character of His holiness, and His holiness cannot tolerate unrepentant sin.

If we who are His people will respond by humbling ourselves, praying, seeking His presence and turning our backs on our sin, then He will be there, ready to receive us, to forgive us, to cleanse us and to reaffirm His love—which was still there even while we were away in the far country of disobedience. Repentance and turning back to God is always met with His gracious forgiveness.

But don't let that be a license to deliberately break His heart—and that is the lesson for us. It is the lesson of how God feels when we sin: it grieves Him, it breaks His heart. Still, He loves us enough to welcome us back into the cover of His grace when we repent. We can be sorry for what we did; we can change our mind and seek God's forgiveness. And He will be there with His grace, mercy and never-ending love—and He'll rejoice over you when you return to Him!

In anthropomorphic terms, God has a "heart"; and in anthropopathic terms, He can grieve. So, before you set out to do something that will cause God to grieve, it's a good idea to ask yourself this: "Is this worth breaking the heart of the God who passionately loves me with an amazing love?"

*And do not grieve the Holy Spirit of God, by whom
you were sealed for the day of redemption.*
EPHESIANS 4:30

## REFLECTION QUESTIONS

1. In Genesis 6:6, the word translated as "repented" in the *King James Version* should be better translated as what other word?

2. Does God know when you will sin? If so, what is His initial response?

3. What is God's response if you do not repent?

4. What is the difference between God grieving and God's anger?

**Notes**

1. Arthur Pink, *Gleanings in the Godhead* (Chicago: Moody Press, 1975), p. 36.

2. Veli-Matti Kärkkäinen, *The Doctrine of God* (Grand Rapids, MI: Baker Academic, 2004), p. 217.

3. Ibid.; p. 216.

4. Benjamin Keach, *Preaching from the Types and Metaphors of the Bible* (Grand Rapids, MI: Kregel Publications, 1972), p. 49.

5. W.A. Pratney, *The Nature and Character of God* (Minneapolis, MN: Bethany House Publishing, 1988), p. 170).

6. Ibid., p. 176.

7. Ibid. Eugene Peterson gives this hermeneutical hint at the grieving mindset of God: "God was sorry that he had made the human race in the first place; it broke his heart."

# 6

# The God Who Rejoices

*The L*ORD *your God in your midst . . . will rejoice over you with gladness.*
ZEPHANIAH 3:17

There is a successful TV game show called *Family Feud* that is hosted
by a friend of mine, comedian Steve Harvey.[1] It is a popular and interesting show in that it pits one family against the other in trying
to answer questions that have been surveyed by a pre-selected panel.
They ask some very strange and unique questions on *Family Feud.*

I've often wondered what their answers would be if contest-
ants were asked questions like, "Name something you would not
expect God to do," or, "Name a feeling you don't think God would
feel," or maybe, "Name an emotion that God would probably never
express." I'm sure there would be all kinds of different answers to
questions like those.

Trying to form a concept of God by imagining Him as having
emotions, passions and feelings is not only a stretch for some people, but it probably comes across as trying to bring God down to
our level. Some would say you should never do that. Yet, not only
does God want to be known, but He also desires that we would
*want* to know Him.

We know God loves and that He is a God of love, and that
everything God does comes out of His love. But we also need to
understand that God has some very unexpected emotions. One of
those emotions is found in Zephaniah 3:14-17:

> Sing, O daughter of Zion! Shout, O Israel! Be glad and re-
> joice with all your heart, O daughter of Jerusalem! The

Kenneth C. Ulmer

LORD has taken away your judgments, He has cast out your
enemy. The King of Israel, the LORD, is in your midst; you
shall see disaster no more. In that day it shall be said to Jerusalem: "Do not fear; Zion, let not your hands be weak. The
LORD your God in your midst, the Mighty One, will save;
He will rejoice over you with gladness, He will quiet you
with His love, He will rejoice over you with singing.

The beginning of this passage says to rejoice with all your
heart. At the end of the passage it says that you are rejoicing to a
God Who Himself is rejoicing. Who would have thought God is a
God who rejoices, who expresses intensified emotions? Answers
on a TV show like *Family Feud* would probably never be "A God
who rejoices." Few people can even imagine a God jumping
around rejoicing, robes bouncing, hands clapping (which are all
images implied by the word "rejoice"). Yet, the Scripture says that
God rejoices—and when God does something, I promise you, He
does not go at it half-heartedly. The revelation is that we don't
have a Savior who cannot be touched or who does not understand
what we are going through. We have a Savior who understands
our emotions, because He has them too.

## When God Rejoices

In Philippians 3:10, Apostle Paul writes that he wants to understand this God with emotions and passions, this God who tells us
to rejoice and rejoices right along with us. Benjamin Keach, in his
book *Preaching from the Types and Metaphors of the Bible*, points out
that there are some characteristics common to both God and man
that are not tainted with the flaws of humanity:

All words which express human affections are first to be
separated from all imperfections, and then understood of
God. When joy or rejoicing are attributed to God, it either
denotes his delight and pleasure in his creatures, or else
his gracious favour and propensity to his church, as men

take joy in things very dear to them [Isaiah 57:5]. There is a joy in God, which exerts itself in gracious effect, but which is infinitely greater than it is in men, or can be thought by them.[2]

Let's take a look at three things that cause God to rejoice with delight and pleasure.

## 1. He Rejoices When He Blesses You

The Zephaniah 3:14-17 passage tells us not to be discouraged and throw up our hands in despair. The phrase, "He will rejoice over you with gladness" (v. 17), is God's attempt to help us understand the kind of exuberance He feels about us. He will rejoice over you in gladness, He will quiet you with His love, He will rejoice over you with singing. Rejoice, by definition, is related to *joy*. The word "joy" means "gladness," "to shine," "to be bright." The Hebrew word for "rejoice" is *samach*, which means "to brighten up," "to make gleesome," "to make merry." To celebrate! Can you picture God leaping and jumping and spinning around in rejoicing? The emotion expressed in the verb *samach* usually finds a visible expression.

In Jeremiah 50:11, the Babylonians are denounced as being glad and jubilant over the pillage of Israel. Their emotion is expressed externally by their skipping about like a threshing heifer and neighing like stallions.

The emotion represented in the verb *samach* (and concretized in the noun *simchah*) is sometimes accompanied by dancing, singing and playing musical instruments. This was the sense when David was heralded by the women of Jerusalem as he returned victorious over the Philistines as recorded in 1 Samuel 18:6. This emotion is usually described as the product of some external situation, circumstance or experience, such as is found in the first biblical appearance of *samach*, in Exodus 4:14, when God told Moses that Aaron was coming to meet him and "when he seeth thee, he will be glad in his heart." This passage speaks of inner feeling that is visibly expressed. When Aaron saw Moses, he was overcome with joy and kissed him (see Exod. 4:27).[3]

Joy and rejoicing are always demonstrative; they're all about jumping and clapping your hands, shouting, expressing jubilation with some noise. It's not a demonstration of being cool—you meditate to be cool. Nor is it an image of a quiet, contemplative, laid-back God. He *rejoices* over you! He's in your midst—He's right where you are right now, rejoicing over you, His special creation.

One version of Zephaniah 3:17 says "the mighty one" will rejoice over you (*ESV*). The role God has when He is rejoicing is that of a mighty God. The word "mighty" is the word for *warrior* or *military hero*. So the God who rejoices is a hero. He wants to be the one you look to as your deliverer. He functions as a conquering warrior who has a track record of military victory. God is not some rookie; He has been in many battles—and won them all. It's important that we picture God as our hero, the warrior who steps into the battle on our side so He can take the glory when He gives us victory—and rejoice over that victory with you.

In the 1960s, there was a cartoon character called "Mighty Mouse." (Okay, so I'm dating myself with this one.) In this cartoon, the main character, Mighty Mouse always showed up when somebody was in trouble. Mighty Mouse was a warrior whose battle cry was, "Heeere I come to save the daaay!" Those words meant Mighty Mouse was on his way to rescue somebody in need. Back in those days, cartoons were not two-hour affairs featuring dancing cakes. "Mighty Mouse" was a short little cartoon; and you knew that whenever somebody was in trouble, sooner or later you would hear, "Here I come to save the day!"—and there came Mighty Mouse.

Obviously, God is not a mouse; He's the mighty God. And no matter how hard the battle is, no matter how bad things are, here comes God to save your day and rescue you. Just when the devil thinks he has all the victory and thinks he is about to stick it to you, you can celebrate with shouts, because God steps in, gives you victory and rejoices right along with you. He is our mighty God. When He sees His children experiencing trouble and being attacked by the devil, He goes into His holy telephone booth mode and comes at the enemy like the mighty God He is, to save you.

Sometimes in Scripture we don't always get the nuances and tone of the text. In Jeremiah 32:41, when God says, "Yes, I will rejoice over them to do them good, and I will assuredly plant them in this land, with all My heart and with all My soul," He is saying that with everything that is in Him, He will rejoice over you and give you victory as a mighty king and warrior.

## 2. He Rejoices When He Disciplines You

> I will make an everlasting covenant with them, that I will not turn away from doing them good (Jer. 32:40).

In this verse, God is saying that He will make a covenant to never stop blessing the people. Then He finishes the verse by saying how He will do this: "I will inspire them to fear me, so that they will never turn away from me" (*NIV*). Watch God's strategy here. He is saying that He will bless them so much that they will fear leaving Him. He will bless them to the point where they will be afraid to leave Him, because there is so much blessing with Him. It almost sounds like a lover who says, "I love you with such a love that will be so pure and joyful that you won't even think about stepping out on me." Have you ever been loved like that?

My wife has made me happy for 35 years. Even if it was in my nature to step out, I'd be too afraid to do anything behind her back.

One time at a restaurant in South Africa, way back when I used to travel by myself, an attractive woman approached me and asked, "So, why are you in town? You want a date?"

Now, I didn't know the lingo. I'm from East St. Louis, so I thought maybe she was talking in code or something. Unknown to me, *Do you want a date?* was a pickup line with prostitutes.

When it suddenly dawned on me what she was up to, in the twinkling of an eye, my wife's face flashed across my mind and I told this woman, "No, no. I can't—I won't. I'm scared."

In that moment, in an instant, God said to me, "It isn't worth it." I wasn't trying to be all deep and holy and spiritual with that woman, I just knew how very blessed I am with my wife.

It's the same with God. He can bless you so much that you'll be afraid to turn away from Him. You can be so close to Him that when the devil throws stuff in your mind or puts temptations in your path that you have a flashback at how good God has been, you remember how faithful He is, how He has blessed you and provided for you. Do you really want to give up all of that for a moment of so-called pleasure? God says He'll bless you so much that you'll be afraid to leave Him. I don't care if they call you a wimp or a chicken or a loser, there are some things to which you have to say, "No thanks. I'm scared to do that, because God has been too good to me!"

So, what if you're tempted to asked yourself, *But . . .what if I indulge myself in sin for momentary physical pleasure?* In other words, "One time can't hurt." How does God respond to that thinking? Deuteronomy 28 answers that in one of the most paradoxical revelations about the character and nature of God:

> And it shall be, that just as the LORD rejoiced over you to do you good and multiply you, so the LORD will rejoice over you to destroy you and bring you to nothing; and you shall be plucked from off the land which you go to possess (Deut. 28:63).

God is saying, in effect, "I rejoice over you. I rejoice in blessing you. I rejoice in delivering you. I rejoice with you. But don't you take Me for granted. Don't hustle me or try to play Me—or else." If you double-cross God, you must not know who you're messing with, because just as He rejoices over blessing us, He'll take the same rejoicing when he whups our behind when we try to pull a fast one on Him. That's a paradoxical statement. God rejoices to bless us and He rejoices to chastise us. The same love in Him that prompts Him to rejoice when you are being blessed is the same love that will love you enough to discipline you when you are being disobedient to Him.

When Hebrews 12:6 says, "Whom the LORD loves He chastens," it is not so much God getting pleasure out of disciplining us as it is that He loves us enough to bless us and protect us, and He loves us enough to chastise us and keep us on the right path. And here's the scary part: You always know when you've deliberately done something wrong, but you don't always know when God is going to chastise you for it.

Did your mother or father ever give you delayed whipping? No matter if my momma was in the choir in the balcony, singing praises to Lord Jesus and doing all her spiritual stuff, if we were messing up in the pews, she would look right at us. She would stop rocking, stare up at the balcony, drill us with a look, and then go right back to singing like she hadn't missed a beat. And I would say, "Oh, boy. We're going to get it now."

Sure enough, when we got home, Momma would say, "Go upstairs and wait for me in the bathroom." As I trudged up those stairs, I would think, *Well, maybe she's just changing her clothes or whatever; you know, getting more comfortable.* And I'd be sitting there in the bathroom, listening to the sound of her cooking, and I'd be smelling the aromas coming off the stove, and after a long time waiting, I'd whimper, "Momma?" As though to say, *Did you forget I'm waiting up here in the bathroom?* It was like, *Is she enjoying this or what?*

Or she'd make us go out to the front yard, where we had a big tree, and she would make us pick our own switch off that tree to spank us with. Pick the weapon she was going to beat us with. One of the worst whippings I got was one day when I picked a little flimsy willow branch that looked like a little buggy whip. Man, she whipped me like she was a crazy woman. Went out and got an old oak branch you could barely lift. I was like, "Momma, this is *me!*— your child, Momma! Your firstborn! This is *tha kid! This is your boy!*"

It was the same enthusiasm with which she would bless us that she would also punish us. She loved us enough not to turn her back when we did wrong. In the same way, God loves you too much to let you get away with doing wrong. It is His desire that you serve Him, that you walk so close to Him, that you're so blessed by Him that you would be afraid to turn from Him and His ways. And I don't mean *fear* in a negative way; I mean fear in the sense of a reverential awe for a God who rejoices when He gives us victory.

### 3. He Rejoices When He Forgives You

God also rejoices when He forgives us. The story in Luke 15:11-32, about the father and the prodigal son, tells about a man who had two sons. One of the sons came to him and said, "Father, give me my stuff. I'm out of here." In recounting the story, we always tend to emphasize the son. But take a closer look at the father in this story. First of all, the father let his son go. He didn't argue, didn't whine, didn't complain. He simply gave his son his inheritance in advance and let him go in peace. Sometimes you've got to love somebody enough to let them go. Some parents try to hold onto their grown kids. Sometimes you've got to love them enough to just let them go. The boy said to his dad, "Give me my inheritance. I'm leaving." Nowhere in that text do you find the father arguing with him. It's as if the father said calmly, "Here it is," and gave the son what he asked for.

So the son went off to a far country. The focus of the narrative seems to be on what happened to the son. The Bible says he went out and spent all of his fortune on partying and wild living. The *King James Version* says the son, "wasted his substance with riotous living" (Luke 15:13). *The Living Bible* says he, "wasted all his money on parties and prostitutes."

Eventually, he hired himself out as a servant, working—of all places—on a pig farm. Good Jewish boy, working around bacon in a hog pen all day long. He'd gone from living high on the hog, to wallowing in a hog pen. The Bible says that when he finally came to his senses, he had a flashback of his father and he said to himself, *What am I doing living in this pig pen?* At least he had enough sense to know he was in the wrong place. At least he knew he was not created to roll with the pigs. Sometimes you've got to tell yourself, "Self, you know you can do better than this. Self, you know you don't deserve to live like this. Self, look at yourself—look at how far you've fallen!"

While all that was going on, the real action was back at home. The picture of the dad who let him go is a picture of the sophisticated Jewish father with long flowing robes of wisdom. Yet, it appears that this gracious father had positioned himself at the top of a long and winding road, hoping for the return of his wayward youngest son. The text implies that day after day, the father would step out onto the porch, look down the road to see if that wayward son was coming home. You don't get the impression that the father ever got impatient or that he was rehearsing in his mind how he would punish his boy. Rather, there was something in that father's spirit that led him, day by day, to go out and look down that empty road.

While he was looking one day, he saw some dust kicking up off yonder on the horizon. The father recognized that this was his long lost son, coming back home. The Bible says that this sophisticated man of decorum lifted up his robes and went running for his son before the son even got to the front gate. The father didn't wait until his boy came trudging up to bow and scrape and explain what he had done. The Bible says the father made the first step in receiving and restoring the son.

And it seems the father had already made up his mind that it was time for celebration because his son had returned. He must have had preparations laid in advance, hired someone to be on standby with music, someone to handle the decorations, the cooking, everything, because the father had it all in place and in action when the older son began to hear the rumblings of partying in the distance. It seems as if the father had prepared in advance for festivities befitting the eventual return of his prodigal son. And now that his son had returned, the father rejoiced.

The Bible says the father went running down the road to meet his son. When he got there, his son fell down and said, "Father, I have sinned against heaven and before you, and I am no longer worthy to be called your son" (Luke 15:18-19). He basically wanted to give his dad the apology speech he'd been rehearsing. But the father ignored him and told his servants, "Bring out the best robe and put it on him, and put a ring on his hand and sandals on his feet" (v. 22). The dad was just glad his son had turned his life around and came home where he belonged.

If you can imagine it, the father and his son were on their way back to the house, where the father had already put the celebration into motion. The closer they got, the louder the music got, because the party had begun. It wasn't time for another punishment. It wasn't time for rebuke. It was time for rejoicing and celebration. He threw a big party and invited everyone to come and see his son, who was dead and is now alive. There was rejoicing in the camp.

## *You* Are God's Joy

I wish you could hear the music of God rejoicing over you. I wish you could recognize the signal to get ready to rejoice when it looks like God has brought you back. Because when God has forgiven you and welcomed you back with open arms, it's time for rejoicing. When God is rejoicing, it's not the time to be too cool and sophisticated and somber. It's also no time to be ashamed of the past. It's time to give God some praise. It's time to rejoice with shouting and dancing. Sometimes God throws a party for you when He gets ready to bless you, to put you in position to receive what He ordained for you.

God rejoices when the wayward returns to Him. He rejoices when somebody gets saved. The word "rejoice" includes the word "joy," the word for *clapping*. Rejoicing includes the word for *shouting*. Make a joyful sound and rejoice. When the Bible says, "God will rejoice over you," the tense of the verb "will rejoice" is imperfect, which means that God *continues* to rejoice. When God says, "Rejoice," He's saying, *Come and join me, and let us rejoice together*. It means that whenever He calls you to rejoice, He's asking you to join in with His rejoicing—He who started rejoicing over you before you even started rejoicing for yourself.

Right now, today, right where you are, you can start rejoicing. Let this message sink into your heart. Rejoice in the God of your salvation. Maybe you're like that son who was out in the far country and you've been away from the Lord for awhile. Maybe there's a decision you need to make, a rededication, a restoration. I pray that you will keep in your mind that if God rejoices over you, then you should rejoice over Him, and you and He can rejoice together over your return to a God whose love never doubts.

God rejoices when He covers you with His favor. He rejoices when you turn and come back to him. You have a mighty God who loves to rejoice over you—and His joy over you should give you joy, because His rejoicing in *you* is proof that in Him there is nothing that you cannot accomplish.

*The joy of the LORD is your strength.*
NEHEMIAH 8:10, *NIV*

## REFLECTION QUESTIONS

1. What are three reasons why God rejoices over you?

2. What is one example of how God has rejoiced over you?

3. Why do you think God that rejoices over blessing you when you obey Him just as much as He rejoices in chastising you when you disobey Him?

**Notes**

1. Harvey is known around the country in television and radio, as well as for his bestselling book *Act Like a Lady, Think Like a Man* (Harper Collins, 2009), which was the basis for the box office hit *Think Like A Man* (Screen Gems, 2012).

2. Benjamin Keach, *Preaching from the Types and Metaphors of the Bible* (Grand Rapids, MI: Kregel Publications, 1972), pp. 40,41).

3. W. E. Vine, *Vine's Expository Dictionary of Biblical Words* (Nashville, TN: Thomas Nelson Publishers, 1985).

# 7

# The God Who Laughs

*He who sits in the heavens shall laugh; the* LORD
*shall hold them in derision.*
PSALM 2:4

We come now to another revelation of a fascinating dimension of
the emotions and passions of God: He is the God who (of all
things) *laughs!* I doubt that many Christians regard the Bible as
something to laugh about. We tend to think of it as containing
pretty serious doctrines, revelations and prophesies. But I'm not
sure how often, if ever, we think of the Bible as a book of laughter.
Yet here the Bible says that we serve a God who sits in the heavens
and laughs. In fact, there are more comedic narratives in Scripture
than there are tragedies.

Laughter is displayed in the Bible in one of at least two ways:
fun laughter and message laughter. Let's look at each.

## Fun Laughter

The book of Ecclesiastes says that there's a time to cry, a time to
weep, a time to laugh (see Eccles. 3:4). So, there is a time when it
is not only in order to laugh (even though it's actually good to
laugh). For example, Psalm 126 talks about the celebration, joy
and laughter when Israel returned from exile, which would be a
time for joyous laughter. And there are "comedic" passages in the
Bible that have to do with things that are purely funny.

We couldn't be blamed for chuckling, for example, at dialog in
the 1 Samuel 21:15 story about when David went before Achish,

king of Gath, and pretended to be insane, and Achish responded, "Am I so short of madmen that you have to bring this fellow here to carry on like this in front of me?"(*NIV*). Or the visual image conjured up by 2 Samuel 10:4, when the Ammonite nobles convinced their leader Hanun that David had sent his men to spy on them, so Hanun seized David's men, shaved off half of each man's beard, cut off their garments in the middle at the buttocks, and sent them away—a funny picture that might cause one to chuckle before realizing the embarrassment caused to David's men. Even the story of Balaam's donkey vocally sassing Balaam is a pretty funny tale. Hollywood would have a field day with scenes like these.

What makes you laugh? What type of things do you regard as funny? Have you ever had a flashback on something that happened a long time ago and you break out laughing and people around you wonder what's wrong with you? Ever looked at something or heard something that you really shouldn't have laughed at it, but you laughed because it was so funny? Sometimes, as the saying goes, laughter is the best medicine.

## Message Laughter

More often, however (and certainly equally as important in Scripture), comedy is used as a rhetorical literary device in opposition to tragedy. For example, the laughter that results from situations that are so shocking that your first response is to laugh. Or laughter from a scenario that contains elements of levity but makes you think beyond the laughter. In other words, it's funny, but there's also a message to it.

I travel quite a bit. I may even travel too much. I have struggled with the ability to say "no" to various invitations I receive. I have had to learn that all invitations are not from the Lord (that's another message for another time). My wife and I used to live outside of Los Angeles in the city of Carson, California. Our home was located near the flight pattern of planes landing at Los Angeles International Airport. One day I returned home from somewhere and my wife met me in our front yard laughing and bursting with anticipation of telling something that happened while I was gone. It seems my son Kendan, who was just a preschooler at the time, was in the yard with my wife when a plane flew over.

Kendan looked up at the plane and said, "Mommy, there goes Daddy!"

She laughed. I laughed. *Ha ha ha ha . . . ha ha . . . ha.* But my laughter quickly faded as I suddenly thought, *They . . . that's not funny!* My son was identifying his father with a plane going somewhere. When I looked beyond the laughter, I realized it wasn't funny. It was rather tragic.

There are stories and narratives in the Bible that are tragic and there are those that are, in a literary sense, comedic. Comedies are, generally speaking, stories that end with unforeseen circumstances. Tragedies are stories that end with the inevitable.

In Scripture, the literary form of comedy is U-shaped. It speaks of a plot or a storyline that starts in joy or pleasantries, but as that story progresses, it descends into some tragic issue. Then the storyline begins to shift and starts to become comedy again, followed by a happy ending. Sometimes the tale ends in a marriage feast, a celebration or a victory over the enemy. Sometimes the story begins at the bottom and then rises to the top, because that's the happy ending.

If you take a broad perspective and zoom wide on the entirety of biblical story, you'll discover that, from a literary standpoint (among other forms), the Bible can be viewed as a comedy that begins with a perfect world and perfect people who then descend into ungodliness. From there, the story goes up and down; and by the time you get to the end of the Bible, you get to a brand-new heaven and a new earth of righteousness. There's a sense, then, that the entire Bible would be seen as a comedy (or even a "tragicomedy").

## Why God Laughs

Psalm 2 is a messianic psalm, which means that the psalmist speaks of prophesies concerning the Messiah. The setting is when God has put His King in Zion. The psalm reads as follows:

Why do the nations rage, and the people plot a vain thing?
The kings of the earth set themselves, and the rulers take
counsel together, against the LORD and against His
Anointed, saying, "Let us break their bonds in pieces and
cast away their cords from us." He who sits in the heavens
shall laugh; the LORD shall hold them in derision. Then
He shall speak to them in His wrath, and distress them in
His deep displeasure: "Yet I have set My King on My holy
hill of Zion. I will declare the decree: The LORD has said to
Me, 'You are My Son, today I have begotten You. Ask of
Me, and I will give You the nations for Your inheritance,
and the ends of the earth for Your possession. You shall
break them with a rod of iron; You shall dash them to
pieces like a potter's vessel.'" Now therefore, be wise, O
kings; be instructed, you judges of the earth. Serve the
LORD with fear, and rejoice with trembling. Kiss the Son,
lest He be angry, and you perish in the way, when His
wrath is kindled but a little. Blessed are all those who put
their trust in Him.

Note that in verse 6 God says, "I have set My king on My holy
hill of Zion." In Israel today, the holy hill of Zion is actually the city
of Jerusalem. Zion was first a small community that was conquered by Israel; when they crossed the Jordan and conquered the
Canaanites, it later became a hill, Mount Zion. That term eventually became a broad designation for the city of Jerusalem.

Jerusalem speaks of God's authority. When God says He set
His King on a hill, He is saying that He has put Him in position.
God has set His King in position of authority on the holy hill of
Zion. In verse 2 it says the kings of the earth and the rulers took
counsel and rose up against God and His Anointed. The Hebrew
word for "anointed" is *maschiach*, which means "messiah." In the
New Testament, *anointed* means "the Anointed One" or *Christos*
(which refers to Christ). God is saying that He set His King, who
is the Anointed One, into position—a position of authority. He is
Lord and King. And the battle begins.

Psalm 2:1 says, "Why do the heathen rage and the people imagine a vain thing?" In other words, What's all the noise about? The
characters in this story are mankind as depicted by the nations.
Psalm 59:8 speaks of God laughing at the enemies who will eventually come to destruction. Psalm 37 speaks of those who have
committed ungodliness, yet are prospering. God laughs at all of
these people because He knows there is no reason to fret over evil-
doers, because they will soon be cut down. In Psalm 37:13, God
laughs at those who are headed for doom. And in Psalm 2, we find
God laughing at the heathen nations because "the people imagine a vain thing." The Hebrew word for "imagine" is "hagah,"
which means "to meditate," to "mutter," or to "murmur." It's the
same word used in Psalm 1 where the people are meditating upon,
devising, plotting a vain thing. The phrase *vain thing* means "a rebellion that cannot succeed." The kings of the earth had set nations and rulers and counsel against the Lord and against His
Anointed, taking up a position against God, setting themselves
against the Almighty and recruiting others to join them.

Watch the flow in Psalm 2, verse 3. They say, "Let us break
their bands asunder, and cast away the cords from us" (*KJV*). The
phrase "let us" implies that they assume they can do just what they
say they'll do. The words "bands" and "cords" do not refer to being a prisoner; they speak of an agrarian culture of plowing and of
the ropes that tie the yoke to oxen to plow a field. It's a picture of
submission to authority. They had decided they no longer wanted
to live under the authority of this King and this Anointed Lord.
They were impatient, they didn't want to do the humility thing
anymore, so they decided to end it and break their position of submission. And they found others to join them, scheming and plan-
ning together to get in a position that would remove them from
the Lordship of Christ.

While all that is going on in verses 1 through 3, in verse 4, God
is laughing: "He who sits in the heavens shall laugh." What might
it sound like to hear God laugh? His laugh had to sound like
something as He sat in the heavens and laughed at their vanity.
Now, here comes the shift in the storyline. When did God laugh?

*Then*—God laughed *right then.* The Bible says He sits in the heavens. To say specifically that God sits in the heavens is a picture of God's sovereign superiority, His supreme position as Creator of the universe. The picture is of God, seated above them in heaven, hearing and seeing what they are up to. As He watches them plot to get away from Him, He suddenly breaks out with a laugh and holds them in derision (see v. 4). Then, verse 5 says He vexed them "in His sore displeasure" *(KJV).* The Hebrew word for "vex" is *bahal,* which means to "tremble inwardly," "be alarmed or agitated," or "hasten anxiously." Basically, God made them scared and confused. The *New Century Version* says, "The one who sits in heaven laughs; the Lord makes fun of them" (v. 4).

Then, in verse 5, the entire atmosphere changes. A few minutes ago, God was laughing. In verses 1, 2, and 3, they want out. In verse 4, God laughs at them. Then verse 5 announces that He is going to speak. But the key to His speaking is *when* He speaks. The revelation is that when He speaks, He is going to speak to them in wrath. As we learned in a previous chapter, wrath is activated anger. Here comes the principle: Laughter always precedes anger, because whenever God stops laughing, that means He's mad. The key is "then." The text does not tell us when "then" is; it only tells us, then He stopped laughing. At first God is incredulous to the point of laughter. Now He's ticked off.

When God looks at your life, what side of "then" is He on? Because whenever He stops laughing at our folly, the next phase is His wrath. His deep displeasure kicks in. In Psalm 2, He laughed at the people because of the impossibility of their strategy. The strategy was, *Hey guys, let's get away from Him! Let's break these cords! Let's be freeee!*

There are several reasons why God laughs. One reason is because of the impossibility of anyone getting away from Him. David gives a revelation of what it means to get away from God when he said, in Psalm 139:8-10, "If I ascend into heaven, You are there; if I make my bed in hell, behold, You are there. If I take the wings of the morning, and dwell in the uttermost parts of the sea, even there Your hand shall lead me." Anyplace I can imagine going, God is there. Where can one go to get away from God? *Nowhere.* You simply cannot get away from God, because wherever you run, He's already there.

Verses 1 through 3 of Psalm 2 are about the activity of men on earth. The laughter in verse 4 is from God's seat in heaven, which implies that they can't hear Him laugh. And because they cannot hear Him laughing at them, they assume their plan will be successful. They assumed they could pull off outmaneuvering God and get away from Him. And God laughed. Our problem is the same: We assume that if we got away without any wrath the last time, then we think we can get away with it the next time.

Another reason God laughs is because of the futility of them lowering their standards. God laughs because no matter if they can deal with it or not, He is not going to lower His standard. The bar is set at the level of Jesus, and you only reach that standard by faith. When you don't reach it, you don't ask God to lower the bar; you try again to go higher than you did the last time.

The question we each need to ask ourselves is, "What side of *'then'* am I on?" Has God begun laughing at what you are doing? His laughter always precedes His wrath. The Bible never tells us when "then" is. But whenever "then" comes, brace yourself, because His anger is next, followed by His wrath.

Listen to what God says when He speaks in His wrath in verse 6: "Yet I have set My king on My holy hill of Zion." Translation: You're too late! They tried to destroy God's authority and live apart from the anointed King, but God says, *It's already done!* The King is already in position. He has been anointed.

In the birth story of Jesus, when Herod decided to kill the babies two years old and younger, his goal was to prevent the King from coming. He didn't realize that as he was devising his scheme to stop the King from arriving, God had already set His King, the Anointed One, in position.

God has placed an anointing on your life. What the devil doesn't realize when he tries to come against you is that, no matter how tricky and slick his scheme might be, he's too late, because the anointing has already been released on your life and he cannot stop you, cannot hold you back, cannot prevent you from becoming all that God has called you to be. You are a part of a royal priesthood, and you stand in the authority that God has given you. The devil cannot stop you.

God serves notice on the enemy against you, so you can declare, "You're too late! I'm here now, and I'm going to be everything God called me to be, because He has already put me in authority in His kingdom." In fact, only *you* can prevent yourself from being all that God wants for your life: by plotting in vain against Him who wants so much for you.

Remember, comedy is a U-shaped literary device that moves tragedy to triumph so that the story always ends on a high note. So now comes the turn in the story. Notice the sequence:

- They scheme against God (see v. 3).
- He laughs and mocks them (see v. 4).
- He speaks to them in wrath and tells them they're too late (see vv. 5-6).
- He tells them who is His Anointed One and what is His (see vv. 7-8).
- He declares judgment on the plotters (see v. 9).

In verse 9, God tells them that they will be broken with a rod of iron and will be dashed to pieces like a potter's vessel. In verses 10 and 11, He gives them a little friendly advice: "Now therefore, be wise, O kings; be instructed, you judges of the earth. Serve the LORD with fear, and rejoice with trembling." Notice the trend: God has gone from watching to laughing to anger to wrath to advice. By verses 10 and 11, He has begun to soften. By verse 12, He displays His grace by calling back the very ones who were trying to get away from Him: "Kiss the Son, lest He be angry, and you perish in the way, when His wrath is kindled but a little. Blessed are all those who put their trust in Him" (v. 12). This is God telling them to stop their foolishness and smarten up, there's still time to return to Him.

In choosing to rebel against the Creator of the universe, the people had taken a position against Him, and it made God angry to the point of warning them that His wrath would bring harsh

555555555

judgment against them. Yet He closes out the psalm with His amazing grace.

## God's Mercy for His Prodigals

Don't ever go to God and ask for justice for yourself. My grandmother used to say, "Mercy suits my case." God wants you to know that there is still time to return to Him. It's part of that same picture of the prodigal son and his father that we visited in the last chapter. The son demanded that his dad give him his inheritance, and he was out of there. And the father stood on that long, dusty road and watched his child walk away from him. Isn't that what God does to us? He loves us enough to let us turn from Him if we choose to. He loves us enough to laugh when we rail against Him. He loves us enough to show jealousy when we've left His love and protection and wisdom—and he even gets angry when we keep on walking. Yet He loves us enough to let us walk away from Him. He loves us enough to say, *Come on back. I'm here for you, always have been, always will be.*

Is God speaking to you today? You may have made some choices out there that took you away from Him—and you knew it. He could have blinked you into oblivion, snapped His finger in judgment, and it would have been over in an instant. But He loves you too much. Can you hear, not His voice of anger, but His voice of grace? *Come on back . . . Come back and worship Me. Come back and rejoice with Me. You've been out there, you've tried it; but if you stay out there, you're going to know judgment, you're going to fall. Come back. I'm always here.* God is telling you today to return to Him. Go on back to Him and worship and praise Him. He will not refuse you.

I pray that God would smile on you and never laugh at you. In Numbers 6:25, Moses says to the people, "The LORD make His face shine upon you." The word "shine" means "smile." I pray that God will smile on you. I pray that you will never position your life so that you turn against Him and cause Him to laugh at the folly of your strategy to try to get away from Him. I pray that you would know His grace that says, *Come on back . . . come home.*

Kenneth C. Ulmer

> *God be merciful to us and bless us, and cause His*
> *face to shine upon us, that Your way may be known on earth,*
> *Your salvation among all nations.*
> PSALM 67:1-2

# REFLECTION QUESTIONS

1. What are two ways in which comedy is displayed in the Bible?

2. What prompts God to laugh?

3. What is one incident in your life that you now realize, as you look back, that God must have laughed at what you did?

4. How did that particular incident turn out?

# 8

# The God Who Rests

*Rest: Inactivity or ease, particularly when it comes after a period of work or effort. Peace or freedom from conflict, disturbance, or trouble.*
HENRY W. HOLLOMAN, *KREGEL DICTIONARY OF THE BIBLE AND THEOLOGY*

I walked into Blackfriars Hall with my heart pumping slightly faster than normal. The excitement of studying at historic Oxford University was almost more than I could contain. I only hoped that my enthusiasm and exuberance wasn't dripping off me like a teenager visiting a *Star Trek* exhibit. Lighting in the classroom was somewhat dim, as one might expect from rooms in a university hundreds of years old.

Blackfriars is a "hall" among the more than 35 colleges that make up Oxford University. At the front of the class was Dr. Marie Henry-Keane, a woman who would leave an indelible imprint on my life. The class was called *Servant Ecclesiology*. The thesis of the class was, "The ultimate model of ministry is the picture and pattern of the life of Jesus, who said, 'The son of man did not come to be served, but to serve.'" This class and the depth and profundity of that declaration would forever alter my entire philosophy of ministry.

Dr. Keane is a Dominican nun, the first one I had ever met. She's the first woman to get a Doctorate in Theology from University of South Africa (UNISA) and the first to join theology faculty at UNISA. We met at Oxford, where the providence of God would cause our lives to cross and my approach to ministry and life would change permanently.

I had learned almost incidentally about the life of the Catholic community of leaders. The annual, seasonal and daily rituals and routines of committed Catholics were part of religious life about which I had not known. My protestant/Baptist/charismatic/Pentecostal spiritual journey certainly included such exercises as prayer, fasting, worship, and what we called "missions," but they were nowhere near as structured as I would discover that they are in the lives of Catholic professionals.

The liturgical calendar, for example, was a foreign concept to my experience with church. I did have a few friends who attended more "high church" churches than mine. And I certainly noticed that the preacher at my friend Bernadette Officer's church (the St. Luke CME church on St. Louis Avenue in East St. Louis, where I was raised) had worn a scarf or tippet around his neck that was sometimes green, sometimes purple and sometimes white (though I didn't find out until much later in life that these colors were related to the Christian calendar). When I was growing up, I had only one practicing Catholic friend: a girl named Esta Jethro, whom I'd met in elementary school.

The highlight of our friendship (which continues to this day) is that Esta and I once danced at the PTA meeting at Washington Elementary School. We did the hottest dance craze of the day, called "At the Hop," recorded by Danny and the Juniors. Everybody was doing "The Hop." I couldn't wait to get home each day to watch *American Bandstand,* live from Philadelphia, hosted by Dick Clark. That's where I learned to do that dance, which amounted to hopping around on one foot or the other to the rhythm of the music.

That night at the PTA, Esta and I were listed on the school program to dance at the PTA. A mock stage area had been marked off in the large room at Washington Elementary that was also used as a gym, an inside play area and a meeting room for assemblies and community events. During the dance, Esta and I hopped from one side of the room and onto the stage area, while many of the people in the audience mouthed the words to the song. "Let's go to the hop (ohh, baby!), let's go to the hop. You can rock it, you can roll it, you can slop it, you can stroll it, at the hop." As I reminisced about that performance at the PTA meeting so long ago with Esta Jethro, I realized that that was the first time in my life that I had connected religion with rhythm. The rhythm of the song as I danced with my Catholic friend was a dot in my life that would, many years later, be connected to the dot at Oxford University, thousands of miles away. Dr. Keane was the kind of professor from whom you could learn more by accident than you would on purpose from most other professors. She deposited two truths into my spirit that changed and helped shape my spiritual life, my theology of the Church, and the priorities of my philosophy of ministry. The first truth was embedded in the thesis statement of the Servant Ecclesiology class that named and described the curriculum. Dr. Keane taught me that the ultimate paradigm for the Church is the model of servanthood displayed in the life of Christ.

The second influential revelation that came from Dr. Keane has helped, haunted and challenged me. In one of her lectures, she said, "Our lives are to be ordered around the rhythms of our relationship with God." She talked about the "order" of her life around specified times of prayer, times of eating, times of serving others, and even times of silence. She shared that as a nun living in a religious community, much of their day was structured around certain rituals and exercises. The sisters got up every day at a certain time. They prayed several times a day at a certain time. They observed a quiet time of silence every day at a certain time.

As I listened to how her life was ordered, I saw her as an incarnation of the wisdom of King Solomon, who said in Ecclesiastes 3:1, "To everything there is a season, a time for every purpose under heaven."

## Ordered Rhythm

A succinct definition of "creation" would be "ordered rhythm." When you examine the account of creation in Genesis, you begin to pick up an almost poetic rhythm in God's creative process. The refrain in the process is, ". . . and the evening and the morning . . ."

were the first day ... the second day ... the third day ... the fourth
day ... the fifth day ... the sixth day. Like a skilled jazz musician
who starts with a musical theme and appears to wander into creative oblivion only to return to the musical home base, or a poet
who weaves textures of innovative storytelling only to return the
familiar rhythmic rhyme established at the commencement of the
literary piece, God too weaves and knits creation together with the
thread of "and the evening and the morning."

The flow of Genesis 1 and 2 reminds me of some of the parties
we used to have when I was in college. The record player would be
blasting some James Brown classic or maybe the Temptations in
their psychedelic period, and just when the house was rocking to
the rhythms of the pulsations of the "component set" (what we
called them before the digital age), somebody would suddenly
break the rhythm by stepping on the electric plug or bumping
against the table that held the record player, and you would in-
stantly lose the groove that had everyone dancing.

That's what it feels like when you read the creation account in
Genesis 1 and 2. "And God said" ... and you knew you were moving into another verse. ... "And the evening and the morning was
the [whichever numbered day was next] ... ok, here we go, into another verse, another day, another verse, another day, and so on ...
and then, *bam!*—when God comes to the seventh day, He breaks
the rhythm, because He doesn't set you up with the now-familiar,
"Then God said," and you don't get the closing lines of the seventh verse, "and the evening and the morning ..."

So, just about the time you think, *Maybe He forgot, and now He'll
get back into it,* your ears and eyes perk up for the missing intro,
"Then God said" (or, assuming you missed it, "and the evening
and morning ..." because God always starts in with something
new). And as you adjust and almost unconsciously prepare for the
ongoing process of creation (anticipating "And the evening and
the morning were the seventh day ..."), instead, He is *blessing* the
seventh day, and the rhythm is broken.

*Whoa, wait a minute,* you think. *He never blessed any of the other
days!* And much like the times we would be dancing at the frat

house and the record had a scratch on it and whatever lyric it got stuck on was repeated over and over, God refers to the seventh day three times (and two more times with the pronoun "it"): "And on the seventh day God ended His work which He had done, and He rested on the seventh day from all His work which He had done. Then God blessed the seventh day and sanctified it, because in it He rested from all His work which God had created and made" (Gen. 2:2-3).

Notice how the rhythm was broken. What had appeared to be a pattern of 1-2-3-4-5-6, had now become a pattern of six plus one (written as "6+", this is a rhetorical poetic device that intentionally highlights the seventh beat as the climax of each of the previous six verses). In other words, it was on the seventh beat that God abruptly pulled the plug. Lights out. Party's over.

## God Rested

Genesis 2:1 contains the revelation that "the heavens and the earth were *finished*"—*boom*, done. Complete. It's a wrap. From then on, it appears to be God's will that the seventh, or Sabbath, day would have no end and would be a perpetual reminder of the conclusion of the creation account. Clearly, God has set us up and prepared us for the ultimate revelation in this text: *God rested*.

As Eugene Patterson puts it in his contemporary biblical paraphrase, *THE MESSAGE*:

> Heaven and Earth were finished, down to the last detail. By the seventh day God had finished his work. On the seventh day he rested from all his work. God blessed the seventh day. He made it a Holy Day because on that day he rested from his work, all the creating God had done (Gen. 2:1-3).

Wait a minute. Whoa. God . . . *rested?* The omnipotent, all-powerful God of the universe, "rested"? I rest when I am tired. I rest when I have exhausted myself doing something. I rest when I need to refresh and get ready for some additional task that will require more energy. I rest for preparation and restoration. I rest after I have expended myself beyond my capacity. But God . . . *resting?* Did He have to lie down for a while and take an actual nap? Did He put his feet up on an ottoman like a mountain or a planet?

Almost every other time I had read this text, I focused on the consecration of the seventh day, the Sabbath day. But when I read this Scripture with a sensitivity to the sensibilities of God, I was gripped by the statement, *God rested*. I must admit that when I try to conjure images of Almighty God, birthed out of my own mundane human imagination, I can imagine Him as a conquering warrior who has never lost a battle. I can also picture Him as a caring potter who loves making living souls called mankind. I can even see Him as a forgiving Father, lovingly chastising His children. But I seldom, if ever, have imagined God reclining on a chaise lounge or slowly swinging in a hammock or changing the number on an adjustable bed.

In actuality, "God rested on the seventh day" does not mean that He closed His eyes and went to sleep, nor is it a picture of God relaxing on a recliner or yawning in a heavenly hammock. In the natural, rest might include closing one's eyes. In fact, my Uncle Morris would fall asleep at the drop of a hat. We didn't know about things like sleep apnea in those days; we just thought he was tired and had nodded off. But when we would shake him or call to him, he would say, "I wasn't sleep. I was just resting my eyes." But I can't quite picture Jesus "resting His eyes" (In my book, *In His Image*, I discussed the "Ever Watching Eyes of God" in a chapter that reveals that God never closes His eyes).

Nor does the idea of *God at rest* suggest that rest is an indifference, for example, toward the actions of Adam and Eve, since indifference was defied by the immediate accessibility of God when Adam and Eve sinned. So, rest is not to be understood as sleeping or indifference.

In addition, God can't rest too much, because Psalm 121:3-4 says, "He will not let your foot slip—he who watches over you will not slumber; indeed, he who watches over Israel will neither slumber nor sleep"(*NIV*). If He does rest, then it must be some divinely symbolic act, for the God I know best is described in Isaiah 40:28 as one who "will not grow tired or weary" (*NIV*).

What does it mean, then, when the Bible says "God rested"? Perhaps we can better understand this text if we look at the two key statements about God in the Genesis 2:1-3 passage. God did two things: He "ended his work" and He "rested." The two words used to describe God's actions are similar in meaning. The word for "ended" means "to complete, to finish"; and "rested" means "to cease from work." Thus, God ended His creative activity and ceased to perform it. This "ceasing" is referred to in Exodus 20:11 as "resting," a term that is similar in concept to ceasing.

But here's the most stunning statement of all concerning this Genesis 2 passage: Hebrews 4:9-10 seems to imply that God's rest from this creative labor *continues to this day*. In fact, in his magnificent book, *Rest: Experiencing God's Peace in a Restless World* (which I highly recommend), psychology professor Dr. Siang-Yang Tan (of Fuller Theological Seminary and Senior Pastor of First Evangelical Church in Glendale, California), describes rest as, "a state of peace, contentment, serenity, refreshment, stillness, tranquility, or calm."[1] Tan suggests that the qualities of rest include:

- Quietness of hearing
- A sober awareness of who we are and who God is
- An ability to let go (and *not* try so hard, even at resting)
- An ability to enjoy leisure, nature and things that do not involve performance
- Reflection
- Trust
- An ability to live from our higher or true self (in other words, to determine our values and live by them)
- An ability to enjoy the moment (for example, not living in the past or the future), "breathing easy," waiting without impatience, and not being impulsive or rash

This is rest from our human perspective. But was it the kind of rest that God did—the kind of rest He models for us? I tend to agree with Dan B. Allender, who, in his book *Sabbath,* wrote, "Rest must have a meaning other than (God) taking a well-deserved break to stoke the fires for the next creative output."[2] Although the word for "rest" means "to cease," Allender says, "Rest doesn't necessarily imply a cessation of activity."[3] Allender comes at the idea from a Jewish perspective, which adds another spin to the activity of God on the seventh day of implied inactivity. Many Jewish commentators say it was on the seventh day that God created *menuha,* a Hebrew word for "rest" but better translated as "joyous repose, tranquility or delight." This term is more like our idea of *happiness.*

## An Example of Resting

Thus, it was on the seventh day of creation that God gave us both permission and an example of resting. It is as if God stepped back from His creation (and from His job as its Creator) and celebrated that creation. He did not take a nap or chill out; rather, He rejoiced in His own creation, separated it from Himself and objectively looked at it now that it was complete and perfect. In this context and definition, God became an example to us for backing off after the completion of a task or assignment, and for resting in the sense of taking delight in (indeed, even celebrating) a job well done.

The institutionalization of the Sabbath became a prominent theme in the unfolding story of God and Israel. For example, when the Israelites were complaining about not having food, God fed them with miraculous manna, yet restricted them in the gathering of manna to six days, with a "rest" on the seventh day (see Exod. 16:23-30). Every seventh day was to be sanctified, made different than, the previous six days. The people were provided "daily bread," but it was gathered on a repeating rhythm of six days on and one day off. Thus, they were instructed to gather twice as much on the sixth day so they could rest on the seventh.

Many people in this fast-paced world wrestle with the demon of workaholism. If you take no vacations, no time for your family, no time to recharge your dwindling energy, then what you might need most is rest. Some people don't know how to slow down and rest. But we have to slow down to rest, and lie down long enough to get the blessing that comes from rest.

One of the most painful scenarios of young couples who break up early in their marriage includes a husband (though not exclusively) who is so busy working to make a living that he never stops long enough to make a life with his family. Couples often drift apart while adorned in the trappings of success. No time to talk. No time to dream. No time to reminisce. No time to plan. Between the hustle and the bustle—the texts, emails, tweets, updating of online social networks and all of the coming and going while climbing the ladder to a self-defined success—what should be a safe and peaceful period of rest becomes a breeding ground for destructive seeds sown by the enemy to kill, steal and destroy the very relationship a couple wants and the peace of mind they seek.

By God resting, He provides for us an example of the concept of the Sabbath as a sign of God's invitation to rest. As the Creator and Redeemer of His people, God rests at creation, not because He is tired, but because *rest is a sign of completion and abundance.* The universe is so well ordered, God's creation so good and His gifts to humanity so generous, that He is able to rest.[4] So, rest from our work becomes one of the characteristics of God that we are to imitate and follow.

I have pastor friends who boast of not having taken a vacation for many years. They seem to say this in an attempt to display their dedication and commitment to their calling. Yet, as Dr. Keane says, "We are to order our lives around the rhythms of our relationship with God." And that rhythm includes rest. For, rest from work is the pattern and image of God Himself.

## True Rest

I am struck by the pattern and rhythm of the life of Jesus: it seemed to be a repeating cycle that was all about *time.* Time with the crowds, time with the disciples, time with the Father; time with the crowds, time with the disciples, time with the Father. Not a bad flow. It tells me that there are times when I stand among the crowds in my life; times when I stand with my family, special friends and loved ones; and times when I stand alone before God. All are in a prioritized rhythm and a pattern of life. God took time to rest with *Himself*. It was a sacred fellowship between the Father, the Son and the Holy Spirit after the "work" of creation—a creation that also followed a pattern:

- The Godhead spoke (Genesis 1:3)
- The Godhead created (Genesis 1:3-31)
- The Godhead rested (Genesis 2:2)

In the words of the old African American preachers, "God stepped out of nowhere, stood up on nothing, spoke to nothing, and told it to be something. Made something out of nothing, placed it from nowhere to somewhere, and told it to stay there!" And then God rested. What a God!

I believe that the idea of God resting is woven within the fabric of His very nature as revealed in several of His divine names. King David had been a shepherd for the sheep of his dad, Jesse, and also became the shepherd of God's sheep, Israel. So David introduces us to God as Jehovah-Rohi, "the Lord our Shepherd." David seemed to learn about the value of rest the hard way. He wrote in Psalm 23:2, "He makes me to lie down in green pastures." The structure of the verb *makes* suggests a causative imperfect action (the Lord *causes* me to lie down). The more common translation, "he makes" me lie down, is right on target. The scene is a common one in the culture of the time.

When David wrote Psalm 23, he may have been having flashbacks to the days when, as a young boy, he tended the sheep of his father. He may have been thinking about those times when he picked a particular place to bed down the flock for the evening. David was an experienced shepherd. He knew that the nature of sheep was that they have a tendency to trot right through the place he had chosen for their rest. So, to make sure they didn't go past the place of rest, David sometimes had to "make" them lie down— maybe by blocking their path; maybe by using skillfully trained dogs that shepherds sometimes use to assist them. There may have been times when he had to physically grab a sheep to prevent it from missing its rest in the pasture. Whatever the situation, the shepherd would "make" the sheep lie down. Likewise, David said the Lord makes us lie down; He makes us rest.

David even suggests that there was a blessing in the green pasture. The shepherd is so intent on the sheep experiencing the blessing of rest in the pasture that he would make the sheep lie down in it, to "wallow in" the blessing. Roll in it. Find comfort in it. Not just taste it, but savor it. *Rest in it.* In the same way, God didn't want David to run past the blessing deposited in the green pasture. He would do whatever it would take to *make* David lie down in the green pasture.

It is no coincidence that God did not rest until after He made mankind. The crown of His creation needed the model of rest as an ingredient in our being and as an imitation of our Maker. On the seventh day, God rested because on our seventh day He knew we would need to rest. That's another clue to this powerful revelation of the character of God: resting is connected to the seventh day—the day that God Himself rested.

In his book *Rest: Experiencing God's Peace in a Restless World*, Dr. Tan states that we "need to have a deeper, more biblical understanding of rest and how to experience or enter into rest—God's rest, in God's way."[5] Dr. Tan goes on to quote the writing of Richard Swenson: "The buzzwords of our lives today are: Busyness. Stress. Overload. The demands of life have far outgrown the resources we have to meet them, leading to . . . The Overload syndrome.'"[6] Tan describes this overload syndrome as "the body's condition when it is 'tightly wound.' I call it 'torque,' and it has to do with the tightness of our muscles and vigilance of our psyche. Healthy rest comes when we allow our high degree of torque to completely unwind. But when torque is at too high a level, it requires an extended period to come down to a restful baseline. Torque isn't easily switched off like a light switch. It only backs off slowly. Many people are wound so tightly they can take months or even years to unwind. . . . The stressful and overloaded conditions of

our world keep most of us in such a high state of torque that we
seldom experience true rest."[7]

## The Benefits of a Pattern of Rest

I can relate to the need for being *made* to rest, because (I confess!) I'm
one of those people who have a hard time resting. My attention span
has always been rather short. In fact, as I look at the dynamics of
my life, if I don't have Attention Deficit Disorder ("ADD"), then I
must at least be borderline. They used to say I was just "hyper." That
was a cool word, but not as classy as having my own three letters—
ADD. I was always on the move. I got bored with things quickly, always needing something more, some new excitement. Looking back
on it, I know the Lord had His hand on me, because I never (or *He*
never) let my unquenchable thirst for more "something" lead me
into drugs or alcohol. It's as if God strategically and providentially
placed some green pastures ahead of me, knowing that if I kept
walking, kept running, kept going toward the green, I would come
upon the next green pasture where, one way or another, He would
*make* me lie down and rest for my own good.

When I was growing up, my mother knew I needed to take
time to relax and rest. In fact, I think my mother and God were in
cahoots with each other to make sure I chilled out. I loved the way
Momma would paraphrase the deep things of God. For "He
maketh me to lie down in green pastures," Momma would simply
tell me, "You need to go somewhere and sit down." She used to
visit California every winter, and became a perennial member of
our church congregation. Whenever it was time for her to return
to East St. Louis, I would have her come before the congregation
and say something of a farewell. Her words always ended with the
same ideas stated in various ways. For example, she would say, "My
son is so busy. Tell God to make my son lie down in green pastures." *Take time to rest.*

My first experience with real rest was onboard a ship during a
14-day cruise from Los Angeles to Hawaii and back. The first couple of days, I felt like what a junkie must feel like trying to quit, cold

turkey. It was like I was in detox. The first thing I realized was that there was nowhere to go—you couldn't just step off the boat. It felt like the walls of the cabin were closing in on me. I think I even had the shakes. I couldn't get into REM sleep. Couldn't focus enough to read. I found no pleasure in joining the dozens of people who would sit on the deck of the ship and gaze out at the endless Pacific Ocean (I never did understand that particular attraction; the scenery never changed—it was 360 degrees of saltwater).

As comforting as my wife Togetta tried to be, I'm sure she was laughing at me on the inside. But after the third day, I felt like someone was gradually turning down the temperature on a thermostat. I felt like I imagine the guys in space capsules must have felt after being launched from Earth faster than a speeding bullet to somewhere out in space, when they finally break through the barrier of the Earth's atmosphere and go into a controlled drifting. *Ahh . . . rest!*

I am convinced that for the remainder of that cruise, my heartbeat was slower. I had never known such sweet rest. In the first few days of that Hawaii cruise, though, I thought I had made a tragic mistake. I'd felt like Maya Angelou's poem "I Know Why The Caged Bird Sings." I do, too. He sings because he wants to get out of that darn cage! And I wanted to get off that boat. But once I hit the "wall" (the breakthrough point beyond the breaking point), I found a level of physical and emotional rest I had never before known. It wasn't inactivity, and it certainly wasn't a zombie-like state. It was an entirely new experience—one I had found almost by accident. I thought back on all I had to go through to get that state of peaceful serenity. Once I'd been *made* to lie down in that (watery) pasture and had realized the benefits, I was able to tell my wife, "This feels good." That taste was enough for me to know there was a real thing called *rest*.

## God: Provider of Peaceful Rest

The God who rested at the completion of creation could also be seen as a dimension of Jehovah-Jireh, the Lord our Provider, who is the source and provider of rest. Or this rest might be seen as a dimension of Jehovah-Shalom, the Lord of Peace. There appears to be a common ground or overlapping of the concepts of rest and peace. They are much like two circles joined at a common area without totally losing their individual attributes. The God who rested is also the God of peace. He is the source of both rest and peace, and the distributor of true rest and peace.

Jesus articulates the ultimate theology of rest when He speaks in Matthew 11:28-29, with the standing invitation to, "Come to Me, all you who labor and are heavy laden, and I will give you rest. Take My yoke upon you and learn from Me, for I am gentle and lowly in heart, and you will find rest for your souls." Although few would argue the eschatological implications of this invitation and its *world-to-come* fulfillment, I believe there is also significance for the here and now.

The coming Jesus in Matthew 11 is related to the resting of God in Genesis 2. These two revelations of God the Father and God the Son converge in the common ground of rest and peace. The Matthew 11:28-29 invitation from Jesus reveals the dual dimensions of a life in Christ: Jesus says, *"come"* and "I will *give you rest"*; and, *"learn of me"* and *"you will find rest"* (emphases added). There is a rest that is "given" after we come to Him, and a rest that is "found" after we learn of Him.[8] Coming and learning is the spiritual process of discipleship. The more we learn, the more rest we find in Him, which in turn leads us to learn to take this rest. This relationship between coming and receiving rest, and learning and finding rest, is similar to the peace that is in God through Christ. Jehovah-Shalom, The Lord of peace, gives us peace *with* God (see Rom. 5:1) when we take His yoke and learn of Him; and He gives us the peace *of* God (see Phil. 4:6-8) as we walk with Him, grow in Him, and trust in Him.

Kelley Varner (who is now in the presence of the Lord) was a dear friend of mine and, in many ways, was one of the men who spiritually mentored me. God gave Kelly a gift of knowledge; his life and writings revealed a prophetic anointing rarely exhibited in the present day body of Christ. In his book *Rest in the Day of Trouble*,[9] Varner reveals in the prophecy of Habakkuk a connection between the God of rest and the God of peace. He sees "the anointed one" in Habakkuk 3:13 as the historic David and the prophetic Christ Messiah who brings salvation to the people of God and to the world. He pictures Habakkuk as having received a theophanic revelation of the One who brings peace and rest in the day of trouble (see Habakkuk 3:16-18). Christ is the Prince of Peace who has become the King and Administrator of Peace.

St. Augustine eloquently overlaid the divine rest that can be found only in God on the innate restlessness in man when he wrote, "Thou has made us for Thyself, and our hearts are restless until they find their rest in Thee." Augustine seems to have been addressing the turmoil of the human heart in saying that our true destiny is to find the rest that is found only in God. When God rested after having completed His work of creation, His rest became both His desire for us and our destiny in Him.

## Refreshed in God

According to the *Dictionary of Biblical Imagery*, "An important part of the meaning of rest is suggested by the mystery of divine rest: it draws a boundary around work and exertion and takes a legitimate delight in celebrating what has been accomplished, without an urge to keep working."[10] The picture of the God who rests also includes the God who is *refreshed*. If we remember that the rest of God is meant to be an example to us, this becomes crucial. In Exodus 31:17, the word for *rest* is the recurring word *Shabbat*; but a new and different word is used for the idea of *refreshment* that accompanies God's rest: *nâphash*. *Nâphash* means that God not only rested, He was also *refreshed*. It suggests a replacement or renewal of energy after doing some sort of work.

What is fascinating about this word as it applies to God is that it is related to the idea of breath or breathing. It is a kind of renewal or replenishment of energy where the energy is figuratively "breathed" back into you. In other words, a "breath of fresh air." When related to rest, *nâphash* conveys the idea of stopping the work or the expenditure of energy and taking a breather in order to have new energy breathed back into you. And here's the kicker: There was no one there but God, which basically means that God breathed into Himself.[11] There was no one or nothing outside of God to refresh God; so God rested long enough to refresh Himself by breathing into Himself. The fundamental revelation is that *the* source of rest and refreshment is God and God alone. Even God can find refreshment—a breath of fresh air—only in Himself.

David offers us some perspective on this principle. The early life of David seemed to mimic the rest/refreshment paradigm that was revealed in the person of God the Father. David had been on the run, fleeing from Saul. In addition to being heartbroken over the terrible relationship with Saul, the man David regarded as a father, the Amalekites had attacked David's headquarters at Ziklag and abducted all the women, sons and daughters of the city—including David's wives Abigail and Ahinoam (see 1 Sam. 30). To top it all off, David was facing mutiny and death by stoning from his own men—friends you would expect to console him, but who were grieved and angry with David for leaving the city unguarded and vulnerable to the attack of the Amalekites.

David was brokenhearted, discouraged and distressed. The term used to describe David's state of mind is "multidimensional," a phrase that combines frustration, anxiety and fear. But it has an even more descriptive meaning: it means to be pressed, to be cramped, to be in narrow straits. By leaving the city of Ziklag unprotected, even though he was trying to do right by going out to fight the Philistines, David had made a tactical error. This well-intentioned move caused personal and corporate tragedy, and David felt like his world was closing in on him. He felt alone, like a failure, betrayed by his own men and saddened over the loss of his family.

I can't even begin to tell you how many times I've been in very tight, stressful, trouble-filled days. I'm sure you can relate to this. Everybody has days, seasons like that.. How do you handle it when it seems the walls of your world are closing in on you? You feel like you're facing the end of your world. If you haven't been there, trust me, one day you will (hopefully not with the simultaneous challenges that David faced). Sooner or later, we all visit the narrow place. When you do, follow David's example: the *King James Version* of 1 Samuel 30:6 says, "David encouraged himself in the LORD his God" (other translations say he strengthened himself).[12] In other words, David did what God did in the creation story. Just as God rested and refreshed himself, David encouraged himself. The connection is that the word "refreshed" means "to renew or restore strength," while the word "encouraged" is widely used to express strength, "to be strong, to strengthen, to be courageous, to overpower."[13] It carries the idea of physical and moral strength. David encouraged himself, strengthened himself, made himself strong. "Encouraged" and "refreshed" are synonymous, yet there is a distinct difference. Notice the complete idea in the actions of David: He encouraged himself "in the LORD his God." The *New International Version* clarifies it even more: "But David found strength in the LORD his God." Notice the strength was not his own. David encouraged himself, found strength in himself, found strength *for* himself *from his God.* He found the strength that God had put in him.

God was refreshed because He breathed into His own being. David was strengthened because he turned to the God-image in him—the God of strength, the God of rest, the Almighty, the God who shares His might and strength and power with His children. God-breathed strength, God-breathed encouragement, God-breathed hope into David.

God will do the same for you. When you stop long enough, when you rest long enough, when you turn to the inward strength that He deposits into your spirit, you encourage yourself. Don't look first to your friends, or for the help of those who walk away from you. Look within, to the rest, refreshment, strength and encouragement that only God—the Holy Spirit in you—can give. Follow David's example and encourage yourself with the God of your salvation. Follow the example of Jesus and make it a habit to find a resting place. Despite His busyness, Jesus took time for retreats from His active life (see Mark 6:45-47 and Luke 6:12; 9:28). He prescribed a similar pattern for His disciples, telling them, "Come aside by yourselves to a deserted place and rest a while" (Mark 6:31). If it helped Jesus, it will help you.

## God Never Sleeps

Psalm 121:4 says, "He who keeps Israel shall neither slumber nor sleep. I love the way Eugene Peterson paraphrases this verse in *THE MESSAGE:* "Not on your life! Israel's Guardian will never doze or sleep." Don't ever think that God gets tired of hearing from you, of blessing you or of loving you.

In Hebrews 13:5, God says He will never leave you nor forsake you. This familiar promise is a wonderful word about God's untiring commitment to His people. The words "leave" and "forsake" mean "to go ahead of" and "to stay behind." God will never go ahead of you and leave you vulnerable to the enemy; nor will He stay behind and let you go ahead all by yourself. God will never get so tired that He has to stop and rest and let you go ahead into the unknown of this life alone. He will never have to stop for a nap and tell you, "You go on ahead. I'll catch up with you after I grab a little shuteye."

In biblical culture, the gods of the nations were often depicted as unresponsive to the prayers and needs of people who called on them, because their gods were seen as often being in need of "rest breaks." The prophet Elijah even joked in 1 Kings 18:27 that the gods of the Baal prophets weren't answering prayers because they were asleep.

The rest of God at the end of the sixth day of creation is the only place in Scripture that says, "God rested." Our God is ever watchful, ever caring, ever mindful of us. He is like a soldier marching guard duty who never needs to go off duty. When I was in the Marine Corps, one of the dreaded duties of a Marine was to walk guard duty. One of the great fears and most punishable acts of a Marine on guard duty was to fall asleep on his watch. You have need for no such fear concerning our God. He does not slumber, does not sleep, and doesn't even need to rest. God will never fall asleep behind the wheel of your life.

I believe you could argue that God's greatest passion of all may have come during that sixth day, when He created mankind, a finale that was immediately followed by *rest*. Imagine how He must have felt, looking out over all He had created.

*Be still, and know that I am God.*

PSALM 46:10

## REFLECTION QUESTIONS

1. What is the meaning of "God rested on the seventh day"?

2. What is "ordered rhythm"?

3. How does this concept of ordered rhythm relate to the Genesis account of creation?

4. What are some of the qualities of rest?

**Notes**

1. Dr. Siang-Yang Tan, *Rest: Experiencing God's Peace in a Restless World* (Vancouver, Regent College Publishing, 2000), pp. 21-22.
2. Dan B. Allender, *Sabbath* (Nashville: Thomas Nelson, 2009).
3. Ibid., p. 27.
4. See Lynne M. Baab, *Sabbath Keeping* (Downers Grove, IL: InterVarsity Press, 2005), p. 42.
5. Dr. Siang-Yang Tan, *Rest: Experiencing God's Peace in a Restless World* Vancouver: Regent College Publishing, 2000), p. 21).
6. Ibid., p. 19.
7. Ibid., p. 20.
8. Kelley Varner, *Rest in the Day of Trouble* (Shippensburg, PA: Destiny Image, 1993), p. 252.
9. Ibid., p. 250.
10. *Dictionary of Biblical Imagery* (Downers Grove, IL: InterVarsity Christian Fellowship,1998).
11. Certainly Adam and Eve were there, having been created on the last day of God's work. But there's no way they could have breathed energy or life back into God, since they were only alive because God breathed life into them (see Gen. 2:7).
12. See the *New King James Version, Complete Jewish Bible* and *THE MESSAGE.*
13. *The Complete Word Study Dictionary: Old Testament* (Chattanooga, TN: AMG Publishers, 2003).

# 9

# The God Who Whistles

*He will lift up a banner to the nations from afar, and will whistle
to them from the end of the earth; surely they shall come with speed,
swiftly. . . . And it shall come to pass in that day that the* LORD
*will whistle for the fly that is in the farthest part of the rivers of Egypt,
and for the bee that is in the land of Assyria.*

ISAIAH 5:26; 7:18

*I will whistle for them and gather them, for I will redeem them;
and they shall increase as they once increased.*

ZECHARIAH 10:8

When I was a boy, I thought it was the coolest thing to whistle.
Some guys and girls used to stick two fingers in their mouth and
whistle. Or they would make a V-shape with their tongue and they
could whistle. It was real cool to do it with no hands. The word
"whistle" means "to make a sound by blowing through your teeth";
it also means "to make a hissing sound." Shepherds would often
train their sheep with a certain whistle sound. Sometimes they
used a mechanical whistle or did it with their hands.

My momma used to say, "Don't get too common with God,"
referring to a degree of reverence that we must maintain in relation
to a Holy God. Yet, it amazes me that, in the context of the passions
of God, there is one emotion He expresses that, if attributed to
Him, would seem to be borderline blasphemy to consider. By that,
I mean it makes God too common to say that He is such an emotional being that He would express His passion in this particular

way. Before I studied the various ways God gets our attention, if somebody had told me that He whistles, I would have responded, "Wait a minute—hold on! You're about to cross the line. God is not that mundane, that humanistic, God is not that common that He would go around *whistling.*" Yet, couched in these prophetic revelations in Isaiah and Zechariah there is an unveiling of the nature of God that might surprise you.

## Heeding the Call

Let's begin with Matthew's account of the Christmas story. (The extended versions of the Christmas story are found in Luke and Matthew.) The first chapter of Matthew connects some dots and unveils a surprising expression of the passionate emotions of the true, living God:

> Now the birth of Jesus Christ was as follows: After His mother Mary was betrothed to Joseph, before they came together, she was found with child of the Holy Spirit. Then Joseph her husband, being a just man, and not wanting to make her a public example, was minded to put her away secretly. But while he thought about these things, behold, an angel of the Lord appeared to him in a dream, saying, "Joseph, son of David, do not be afraid to take to you Mary your wife, for that which is conceived in her is of the Holy Spirit. And she will bring forth a Son, and you shall call His name JESUS, for He will save His people from their sins." So all this was done that it might be fulfilled which was spoken by the Lord through the prophet, saying: "Behold, the virgin shall be with child, and bear a Son, and they shall call His name Immanuel," which is translated, "God with us" (Matt. 1:18-23).

Matthew's account says that there shall come forth a child from the womb of a virgin, that this child shall be called Jesus, and that they shall also call Him Immanuel. Whenever you hear or see a name that ends with "el," you know that somewhere in that name is a reference to God. So, Immanuel, the name for Christ, is broken out like this: *Immanu* is a declension of the term "with us," and *el* means "God." Thus, *God with us* or *God among us.*

It's interesting to note, however, that nowhere in Scripture are God or Jesus addressed as Immanuel. This is because the *"with us-ness"* of God is not so much an approach or an address as it is an existential experience. In other words, we don't call him "God with us"; we experience God with us. The Bible also says that the birth of Christ was to be a fulfillment of the prophecy spoken by the prophet in Isaiah 7:14: "Therefore the Lord Himself will give you a sign: Behold, the virgin shall conceive and bear a Son, and shall call His name Immanuel." This coming forth of the Son shall be a sign—the sign revealed in His name that He is "God with us." So the prophet declared hundreds of years before Bethlehem that the child shall come forth bearing the name *God with us.*

Now to Isaiah 7:18: "And it shall come to pass in that day ["in that day" is often used as a period of time; so it means that something is going to happen within the context of the child Immanuel] that the LORD will whistle." The Lord will *what?* The eternal God, the Great Creator of all . . . *whistling?* This God who was in the beginning, this God who has always been, this God who was before the beginning began to begin, this God who is eternal—is *whistling?* I sometimes struggle with these anthropomorphisms. I strain, for example, with what it might sound like if God were laughing, or angry or jealous. Now we have the same God whistling. Was it a shrill, ear-piercing sound? Was it a whistle with a vibrato, like skilled people who whistle songs? Was it like a "wolf call" that rowdy men use to get the attention of women as they pass by? We don't know. We just know that God whistled.

This text in Isaiah 7 indicates that the whistle of God is *gathering.* Isaiah 7:18 tells us that God will "whistle for the fly that is in the farthest part of the rivers of Egypt, and for the bee that is in the land of Assyria." Flies represent the nation of Egypt (flies were common in Egypt—one of the ten plagues was of flies), and bees symbolized the nation of Assyria (bees were common in Assyria).

In other words, God is preparing to gather those two nations to come against a disobedient Israel to turn them back to Him. And the method by which He would do it was that He would whistle in order to gather them.

People whistle to get attention or when they're happy, or even when they're working. Traffic cops use whistles to give instructions, to get our attention and to give us direction as to which way to go or not to go. In the Bible, whistling means "to bring to a place," "to call them for direction," "to call together," "to call to get the attention of." It means that God is about to get their attention under His authority. He's going to instruct them to do something. In Isaiah 5, God whistles to gather nations. Think of God's whistle as a sovereign summons.

In 1876, a man named Sir Francis Galton, who invented the "Galton whistle" (a device for testing the audio range of humans and dogs), once performed an interesting scientific study on the audio range of human beings to see how well we can hear.[1] Galton conducted an experiment where he raised audio tones higher and higher to see how high the sound would go until humans could no longer hear it. To do this, he used a whistle that didn't blow. Instead, his whistle was fitted with a plunger that adjusted the length and amount of air passing through the whistle. The shorter the pipe, the higher the tone. Galton discovered that there are certain tones that young people can hear that older people can't detect. When we are older, our hearing somehow narrows and we can't hear the same levels and tones we were able to hear when we were young. (There are ring tones made just for teenagers' mobile phones that are set at a tonal frequency that older people can't detect—I can imagine teenagers all over the country, getting ring tones in class that teachers can't hear.)

Galton also discovered that there's another level that humans can't hear at all, but certain animals can hear (and even then, smaller animals can hear it better than bigger animals). In other words, you have to be able to hear at another level. It doesn't matter how hard the whistle is blown; if you're not hearing the proper level, you can't hear it. It is significant that it's possible for a person in the same room to hear a tone and get messages from a certain sound dimension, yet a person next to them is unable to detect the sound at all. And it is from that message, delivered in a specific sound dimension at another level, that people get instruction.

The Bible says that Isaiah gave the prophecy. It is significant that God called Isaiah to deliver this prophecy, because this is the same Isaiah who saw the glory of the Lord:

> So I said: "Woe is me, for I am undone! Because I am a man of unclean lips, and I dwell in the midst of a people of unclean lips; for my eyes have seen the King, the LORD of hosts" (Isa. 6:5).

In this verse, Isaiah is saying that he is a man of sin, he lives among a people of sin, he's a man of uncleanness, and he traffics in unclean circles. Yet, in the very next chapter, in Isaiah 7:3, God calls this same man—essentially giving him a whistle that it seems no one else heard: The whistle for service, because God wanted to use him.

I love the phrase in Isaiah 6:8 when God says, "Who will go?"; and Isaiah responds, "Here am I! Send me." Most of us would have replied, "Here I am. But send him. You don't really want to use somebody like me for this gig, Lord. You need somebody who has a great testimony, a history of holiness and righteousness. But don't send me—I'm all messed up." To that, God might just respond with something like, "You're *exactly* the kind of person I'm looking for. I want to use *you*."

God told Isaiah to go and tell them that the child's name shall be Immanuel—the Lord is with us. Yet in order for Isaiah to be obedient and deliver the prophecy, it was required that he say, "The Lord is with us." The first person God called to tell the world that Immanuel is with us was this Isaiah who had already noted how sinful he was—and may have felt better saying, "The Lord is with *you*." But he was also the same man who had previously replied to God, in Isaiah 6:8, "Here am I! Send me." Thus, the revelation in God's instructions to Isaiah was that he was forgiven, so get on with it, don't dwell on it, don't mope, just do it. He heard God's whistle and heeded God's call.

Do you hear God's whistle when He calls you? If someone has determined that your life is so messed up that even God can't fix it, then God would likely reply to that something like, *"HHHREEET!* [that's my spelling of a whistle sound], Come here anyway—I still want to use you. You tell them the Lord is with us." Because, by definition, that means He's with you, too. Sometimes we have to learn to encourage ourselves. You may be good at encouraging others, but you've got to learn how to encourage yourself when nobody's around to read Scripture to you to pump you up. God whistles to tell you that He still wants to use you, that He's able to make something out of what you might see as a mediocre life. He is more than able to take the broken pieces of your life and make something significant out of them.

By instructing Isaiah to tell them I Am is with us, God wanted Isaiah to know that He still wanted to use him. And God wants you to know that He still wants to use you, too. He made you—He sees amazing value in your life. And He is never wrong. All you have to do when you hear Him whistle is say, "Here I am, Lord. Use me."

## A New Testament Whistle

Let's go back to the manger, back to Matthew, when God called Mary and Joseph. It is fascinating how God navigated the circumstances of their lives. I love the story about the inn. It gives the impression everyplace else is full, so they go to this place. But they still can't get in, because it's all booked up, too. Finally, they find a place where the proprietor tells them there's a place out back they can stay. It's not fancy; only a manger in a stable, but it is dry.

Have you ever been trying to get through some doors that were closed in your face? Do you know what it's like to try to find a spot over there, but they wouldn't let you in? Try another place, and they say, "Sorry, we don't need you"? Do you know what it's like to keep knocking on doors, and no doors open?

God called a Mary and a Joseph who knew something about closed doors, who had faced the frustration of having doors closed in their faces and people gossiping behind their backs. God called the Mary who had, for nine months, been living with shame. Being an unwed mother (technically, a single parent) with the ridicule and criticism of those days put her in a precarious situation, because people probably assumed she was in her condition due to disobedience—a perception that cost Mary a great price.

Mary actually became ashamed while she tried to walk in obedience. People pointed the finger at her because she hadn't followed the trend of the day. She had a stigma put on her just for trying to walk in obedience. I'm sure there were places where they didn't even allow her inside. They saw her coming and may have wagged their heads because she had to live nine months with the shame of being a Jewish, pregnant, unwed mother in the first century.

Do you know what it's like to try to be obedient, and that obedience cost you a price? Yet, God called Mary and she heard His whistle and heeded his call. The other side of the story is what Joseph also endured. Joseph knew what it was like to be embarrassed due to his obedience. The fellas probably talked behind his back down at the temple. I'd bet everybody raised their eyebrows about how he was stuck with that "young woman, Mary." To top it off, rumor had it that the child Mary was carrying wasn't even Joseph's. Oh yes, Joseph knew something about living with embarrassment and shame, too.

## A Walking Miracle

When God called Mary and Joseph, Mary came bearing a Miracle. God called them to the manger, having supernaturally placed Someone inside her that would bring Him glory. Mary herself was a walking miracle. When people saw her walking down the street, they had no idea they had just passed by a miracle: The unborn Messiah.

There are people today whose lives are a testimony to the greatness and goodness of God. In fact, you may not realize it, but there are miracles in your life. The person who lives next door to you doesn't realize who they're living near, child of God. God is calling you to celebrate what He's about to do in your life. If it has not yet come forth, then hold on, it will. Don't worry about the folks around you who didn't hear His whistle to you. You just focus on being everything God called you to be. He called you to be a miracle.

God also whistled and shepherds came. The life of a shepherd was characterized by danger and loneliness. They were often robbed, attacked and ambushed as they led their sheep across the fields. It was a truly lonely existence. Have you ever been truly lonely? When God calls shepherds, He calls some lonely folk. When He called them, He was calling them to the one who is named *God Is With Us*. He calls those who feel alone to tell them that they may feel lonely, but they're not alone. Lonely is a sense of isolation and rejection. It's those seasons where you play it off and become skilled at faking it until you start making it. You've got the right smile, the right greeting. But there's a loneliness and a void.

I can struggle through loneliness when I realize I'm not alone. When I hear God say to me, "Come here. I am with you," I can make it through the rough spots, because He reminds me that I am not by myself. But what about the times when you don't recognize that God is there with you? Have you ever been in a room and you couldn't see anybody, but you sensed somebody was there with you? Sometimes that's the way God is. You might not be able to see Him all the time, but every now and then, He'll tug at your heartstrings and you suddenly know that while you may be there by yourself, you get a feeling that God is with you and everything is going to be all right. There's no change in your circumstances; yet a sense of peace and comfort overcomes you. That's because you just heard God's whistle.

God called Mary and Joseph, even in their loneliness. Then, sometime after Bethlehem, He blew the whistle again when Herod had given the order to kill all the babies two years old and younger in his twisted effort to eliminate the Messiah. In the second chapter of Matthew, the wise men appeared, following a star. These magi were skilled. They traveled by the stars, reading the heavens, and when they saw a star that was brighter than any of the others, that was God's whistle, and they followed it. They had seen stars before, but this one was special. It gave off a light so exquisite and bright that the lights that normally appeared bright in the heavens before this one came, now looked dim in comparison.

You may have seen such lights before—things that once looked appealing. Perhaps you followed certain lights because they looked so bright. Some people settle for a light that's flickering. Some settle for a light with low wattage. But when the light of Christ shines in your life, His light is so bright that it causes you to realize that the lights you had thought were bright before don't shine with nearly the luminescence of *this* light—and now you want the *real* Light.

In John 3:19, the apostle wrote, "Light has come into the world, and men loved darkness rather than light." That verse amazes me. John says that the people preferred darkness over light. Have you ever settled for darkness? When you've been in the darkness for awhile, your eyes become accustomed to the dimness, and even a dim bulb can appear bright. But it's not that the darkness has lessened; it's that your eyes have become used to dimness. And when a bright light comes along, you realize that you had previously been living in darkness.

In Matthew 11:28, Jesus says, "Come to Me, all you who labor and are heavy laden and I will give you rest." He calls, He whistles for, the restless, scattered spirit, because He is going to redeem them. Zechariah 10:8 says, "And they shall increase as they once increased." He called them not only to be saved, but to be blessed and to increase.

How dare I say "increase" in economically trying times like these? You've heard the news reports, but somewhere you've got to decide whose report you want to believe: God's or the world's. God wants to take you to a place to position you for a blessing. It's the idea of gathering you from wherever you are, and bringing you over to where He is. You can't receive His blessing over yonder. He's whistling, telling you to come follow Him. Maybe He's whistling to you to let you know He still wants to use you. Maybe you've been saying, "I want to be used by You, Lord, but I've messed things up." To that, God says, "I still want to use you." It might cost you something while you walk in the destiny God wants for you, but the cost will be far less than the benefits.

God whistles to those who are looking for the light. The whistle is His sovereign summons, His way of getting your attention so He can give you direction. Do you hear God's whistle? Your season for being over there might be coming to an end, and God is calling you to leave there and come over next to Him, because your redemption is where God is. And He has mighty plans for those who hear His call.

> *But you are a chosen generation, a royal priesthood, a holy nation,*
> *His own special people, that you may proclaim the praises of Him who*
> *called you out of darkness into His marvelous light.*
> 1 PETER 2:9

## REFLECTION QUESTIONS

1. People whistle to get attention or when they're happy or when they're working. Traffic police officers use whistles to get our attention and give us instructions as to which way to go or not to go. But why does God whistle?

2. How did God "whistle to" or call Mary and Joseph?

3. When was a time when you heard God's "whistle" call to you? How did you respond?

**Note**

1. Sir Francis Galton, *Inquiries into Human Faculty and its Development* (London: J. M. Dent & Company, 1876).

# 10

# The God Who Sings

*The* LORD *your God in your midst, the Mighty One, will save;*
*He will rejoice over you with gladness, He will quiet you with His love,*
*He will rejoice over you with singing.*

ZEPHANIAH 3:17

I love the revelation that God rejoices over His children with actual singing. We, in turn, are encouraged and called upon in Scripture to sing unto the Lord. Imagine what kind of world it would be if we were all speaking to one another in psalms and hymns and spiritual songs, singing and making melody in our hearts to the Lord, as it says in Ephesians 5:19. From the beginning of Scripture to the end, there are revelations of the presence of music. At creation, the Bible depicts the morning stars singing together and the sons of God shouting for joy (see Job 38:7). Some say the morning stars are symbolic of angels expressing joy of God's creation.

At the other end of Scripture, in Revelation 5:13, there is a magnificent picture of the scene around the throne of God, with the elders, angels, seraphim and cherubim bowing and praising God and singing to Him who sits on the throne and to the Lamb. Over and over again, from the Psalms to Revelation, the Bible talks of singing songs unto God.

Songs have always marked critical points in the history of Israel. As God delivered the Hebrew nation through the Red Sea, a woman by the name of Deborah led the celebration with a song. King David is seen as a musician anointed by God. In fact, 2 Samuel 23:1 calls David "the sweet psalmist of Israel" (or, in the *New International Version*, "Israel's singer of songs"). The early Christians would often gather together, and part of their gathering was dedicated to singing songs.

In the Bible, music is used to express just about every emotion you can imagine. There are songs of joy, songs of sadness, songs of victory, songs in the midst of battle, songs of jeering and mocking. It's interesting that there are three listings of gifts in the New Testament. There's a list in 1 Corinthians 12:7-10, another one in Romans 12:4-8, and one in Ephesians 4:11-12. Most scholars (particularly Old Testament scholars) would include the gift of music in the lists of spiritual gifts. Music is a part of the very fabric of the people of God, and it is God who is always behind their music. For it is God who gives gifts, and one of those gifts is the gift of music. When He moves in the heart of His people, they come forth with song. The book of Psalms is literally a hymnbook (the word "psalm" means "song") with 150 songs (or psalms) that make up the book. And God Himself gets triple music credits, because He is a producer, composer and singer.

In this chapter, we are going to learn about the God who is presented as a singer who, the Bible says, sings over us. We are going to look at several revelations about His singing nature and the emotion and passion that brings God to sing.

If you are familiar with music artists, or if you follow any of the music awards (Grammys, American Music Awards, MTV Awards, BET Awards, etc.), then you know that one of the keys to the success of many a music project is not only the art, skill and talent of a musician or singer, it's also the producer. The producer is the one who is behind the scenes of the product, who selects the songs, often arranges them, oversees the recording sessions and sits at the mixing board during the recordings. Thus, the producer is the one who is more involved with the project on an all-inclusive creation level than even the musicians themselves.

I suggest to you that, from a musical perspective, God is a producer. First Kings 4:29 says that God gave Solomon wisdom, exceedingly great understanding, and largeness of heart like the sand of the seashore. In 1 Kings 4:32, we learn that Solomon spoke 3,000 proverbs and that his songs numbered 1,005. But it was God who was behind Solomon's talent, producing within him the ability to write songs, proverbs and psalms.

Most people probably think King David wrote all the psalms. In fact, Solomon did write at least two of them. One of the psalms of Solomon is Psalm 127, described as "song of degrees" (or "ascents"). The Hebrew word for "degrees" is *ma'alah*, which means "a journey to a higher place." So here is Solomon, who built the temple and lived out the vision and dream of his father David, who also writes this psalm. You can almost envision him strumming a lyre or another instrument as he sings lyrics that tell that unless the Lord builds the house, if God is not the one who is building the house, no matter how much labor you put into it, your efforts are in vain. There is a lesson being taught in this song, and behind that lesson is God, for God taught it to the one who sang it.

God has put a song in your heart too. He has taught you many things throughout your life—lessons and instruction, songs of truth—that He produced and placed within you as He teaches you throughout your life. God is behind the incident that brought forth the song of the lesson. If you ask composers where they were and what they were going through when they wrote a song, most will tell you about a sequence of events or of an incident that led them to write the song. For example, a multiple-Grammy winner singer named Adele wrote a song about how she was in a relationship with a man and how they broke up. She wrote a memorable and poignant song about the incident, telling the circumstances behind the song, the lesson she learned, the emotions she felt.

I have several friends who are composers. One keeps a note pad beside his bed because he often gets ideas and lyrics for songs while he sleeps and often wakes up to write down what he hears. I have another friend who used to keep a tape recorder (I'm sure he keeps some more modern recording device now) at his bedside to record what has come to him in the night. The idea is that God often teaches and speaks to us through music and song. God releases into our lives lessons that we learn, truths we must not forget, and incidents where praise is called for. Their purpose is that we remember and hold on to these life lessons. God is behind them, and God alone is the producer and composer of all such songs.

## Song: "Teach it Forward" Discipleship

In Deuteronomy 31, when God revealed to Moses that he would soon die, He asked Moses to bring Joshua to the tent of meeting where He would commission Joshua to succeed Moses as leader of the children of Israel. God said, "Now therefore, write down this song for yourselves, and teach it to the children of Israel; put it in their mouths, that this song may be a witness for Me against the children of Israel" (Deut. 31:19). God was about to give Moses the song that is found in Deuteronomy 32. God told Moses that the song was to be sung for God, Moses was to write it down, and he was to teach it to the people so that they would not forget it.

I wonder what the song sounded like as God taught it to Moses. One of the challenges we face when reading Scripture is that we don't have the soundtrack. We can't always clearly discern the feelings and emotions or the "voice quality" of the text. We can't hear the audio. We have the lyrics without the melody.

I have always been fascinated by music composer teams. You don't always know which partner contributed the lyrics and which one produced the music and melody and harmonies. Joe Westmoreland and Charles May, two popular gospel music composers who are now with the Lord, were known for their powerful, Spirit-filled, prolific compositions. Joe came up with the lyrics and brought them to Charles, who put them to music. In the pop world, Ashford and Simpson, who wrote "Ain't No Mountain High Enough," collaborated on that smash hit. In earlier years, George and Ira Gershwin collaborated on one of the timeless musical classics, "*Porgy and Bess,*" which was the product of Ira's lyrics and George's music. I would love to have heard God's original melody to the song Moses recorded in Deuteronomy 32. I wonder what it felt like for Moses to be taking music dictation from God. I wonder if the Lord gave him harmonies. Three part? Four part, to include a bass line? That must have been fantastic. The lyrics of the Deuteronomy 32 song tell the story of God's favor and His deliverance and righteousness toward the Israelites who, as it says in verse 5, had corrupted themselves and became a "perverse and crooked generation." God was telling them He didn't want them to forget this, so He put this truth in a song. That way, they would never forget how He felt about what they had been doing. *I don't want you to forget this*, God was telling them; putting the truth in a song to aid them in remembering the lesson through it. It must have been fantastic to hear in your spiritual ear the Lord declaring his love for His people in the words of a song. Our God. The great lover. The great singer.

When you look closer at this idea of the Lord as singer-composer, you see something else. This is actually a discipleship process similar to what Paul had instructed Timothy: "The things that you have heard from me among many witnesses, commit these to faithful men who will be able to teach others also" (2 Tim. 2:2). That is discipleship. Even in music, we understand that God releases a discipleship principal. God told Moses that He was giving the song to him. He was not to keep it to himself, but pass it on to people; they in turn were to pass it on to their children. God was doing this because He didn't want them to forget when they got prosperous and when they got to the other side of struggle and the thick of the battle was behind them. He wanted them never to forget how He had blessed them and pulled them through the tough times. Because when the load lightens, people tend to forget two things: the God Who brought them through the trials, and the God Who is still their God during the good times. The vehicle God chose to help them to remember what He had done for them was *music* and *singing*. He told Moses, "This song . . . will not be forgotten in the mouths of their descendants, for I know the inclination of their behavior today, even before I have brought them to the land of which I swore to give them" (Deut. 31:21). So Moses wrote this song the same day and taught it to the children of Israel.

The reason for using song as a vehicle for discipleship teaching is that it is often easier for us to learn the melody and lyrics to a song than to memorize a passage of text. Song melodies and lyrics stick in our head more easily than rote memorization of a list or a page filled with words or instructions. For example, if I told you to recite the alphabet, chances are pretty good that you wouldn't simply say the 26 letters in order from A to Z, because, like most people, you would probably sing the "ABC song" instead. That's what helped most of us to learn the alphabet in the first place; the song imprinted the memory of the letters into our mind permanently and in proper order. That's how God taught the people to learn about Him and His commands, instructions and ways (in the same way we today learn the "ABCs" through a simple song).

The principal is that God creates and composes a song. Then He tells us to take the song and learn it, and then we pass it on to others. Sing it to them and thereby teach it to them. Thus, as it says in Deuteronomy 31:22, Moses took what he learned from God and taught it to the Israelites so that they might teach it forward, releasing it to the people so that they would then pass it on to their children and their children's children, to aid them too in learning what the song was teaching that was important that they learn.

At our church in Los Angeles, the praise team sometimes teaches the congregation a new song. The church members learn, within the song, new truths and principles about God. We learn it and sing it and teach it to others. It's the same principle with the disciples and prophets. God told Moses to take the song down verbatim, the way He dictated it. Don't improvise, don't get creative, don't put in words God never said, don't leave out any words. The story began with God, then went through Moses, who was then held accountable for releasing it forward. Don't rearrange it. Just tell the story like God gave it. There was a story in the song—a story of experience that the people came through by God's power. The discipleship principal in music.

What is your song, your story? What has God taught you, shown you, revealed to you, brought you through, that you need to remember and tell others about? What ever it is, don't sit on it. It's a story of the battles God has rescued you from and pulled you through. God never blesses you just for you alone. He blesses you so that you may turn around and bless others. There's a line in an Oscar Hammerstein song that goes, "A song is not a song until you sing it." Are you singing whatever song lesson the Lord put in your heart? Are you releasing that story and giving God credit and glory? Sometimes the song God gives us is a song in the night. Sometimes it's a song in a storm. Sometimes it's a song in a battle. A song is but a story lesson that God releases into your life—but you've got to *sing it*. You need to *tell it*. It's your story. Writers will tell you that if there's a book in you, it has to come out of you. Singers will tell you that if there's a song in you, it's has to come out. They write because they're pregnant with a story, a word, an idea, a song, a testimony, an experience. When God puts His song into your spirit, it has got to get out.

It's amazing how many books or songs are never read or heard. When God gives you a song or a story, it's never meant only for you, and nobody can really tell your story but you (they certainly can't tell it the way you can). You have a story. It's your story. It's an original story, a unique point of view, a personal, internal revelation from your experience, and nobody can tell that story but you. If you don't tell it, nobody can learn from it.

## God's Songs of Love

The pattern is that God positions Himself as the composer behind the song, then He flips to being the producer of the song. When God sings, His song is always an expression of His love, for He loves you with an everlasting love.

In Zephaniah 3:17, God is presented as a singer, as the God who will rejoice over us and quiets us with His love. Isaiah 62 portrays a beautiful (though painful) picture, because of what has happened to bring the Israelites to this place. God's singing comes together with His rejoicing in a love song He sings over the people:

> As a young man marries a virgin, so shall your sons marry you; and as the bridegroom rejoices over the bride, so shall your God rejoice over you (Isa. 62:5).

This is a love song likened to a young groom passionately in love with his young virginal bride. The verse says God rejoices over him like a groom. Have you ever seen young love? I mean young, syrupy, sticky, dripping-off-of-you, get-a-room type of love? God says His love for you is like that of a young groom passionately in love with his new bride. That is significant because of the historical position of the text. The significance of God's love, His rejoicing in song, is in the placement of this particular passage: the text is referring to a time period *after* Israel had cheated on God. So, in this instance, when God says in Isaiah 62:5 that as a bridegroom rejoices over his bride, so will God rejoice over you, it's not a picture of a wedding day, but of *restoration*. It's a picture of forgiveness. This is a love song being sung by one who has been betrayed by their lover, cheated on by the one they love (in this case, with idols). It's an image of two lovers making up after one has broken the heart of the other (as opposed to a remembrance of the great day when they first stood together to make their vows). This is a time after a lot of things have happened between them. Love that had been so passionate in the beginning has by now gone cold. The Bible says Israel had walked away from her loved One, chased after other lovers, whored after other gods all the way from Exodus right up to this chapter in Isaiah. Yet, here God lets Israel know that He still loves them just like He did when He first married her, before she messed up. God sings a song of love so passionate that even after being hurt and bruised and crushed and deserted, His love is still there for them. It's an emotional love song that pictures a couple who have been estranged from each other because one chose to go after other lovers. Yet, God says he loves her the same way He did on the first day she said, *I do*. That's tough, hang-in-there, unconditional love—the kind of love God wants us to learn to feel and to express for one another.

Zephaniah 3:17 relays the message of God's rejoicing songs of love this way: "The LORD your God in your midst, The Mighty One, will save; He will rejoice over you with gladness, He will quiet you with His love, He will rejoice over you with singing." The prophet is saying that God is a strong warrior among them, there to save them and happy to have them back. Isaiah 65:19 describes God's forgiving love like this: "I will rejoice over Jerusalem and take delight in my people; the sound of weeping and of crying will be heard in it no more" (*NIV*). This is a picture of a groom cuddling a lover who betrayed Him who returns weeping with repentance. God embraces this lover and tells her He's happy to have her back. The Zephaniah 3:17 portrayal can be likened to a wounded lover holding the one who has crushed him, his heart filled with forgiveness. Yet in spite of what happened while she was away, he is rejoicing now that she has come back home.

In the *New American Standard Version*, Zephaniah describes this love in this way: "He will be quiet in His love" (Zeph. 3:17). The key is silence; this a silent love. God is not saying a word. He's not condemning, He's not accusing. He's just complacent to have her in His arms again. Which means He never throws it in her face what she did when she left Him and went away. It's a picture of two lovers who have been through some stuff together, but are so settled in their love that they don't have to say a thing.

There's an interesting compliment in two versions of this verse. The *New Living Translation* says, "He will calm all your fears;" the *New King James Version* says, "He will quiet you with His love." The *New International Reader's Version* combines the two into, "The quietness of His love will calm you down." Here's the idea: It is the calmness of God's presence, being content with His presence. There's a depth of contentment that calms the returning lover. Yet, it is as though the love He feels for her is so strong, so powerful and so potent that He goes from silence to song. The word for "song" implies an *eruption*, a *breaking out in singing*. It's as though He has caressed her, forgiven her, received her, is glad to be in her presence, and the song just rises within Him.

I wonder what might have gone through her mind as she heard the melodious strains of His love and forgiveness, knowing what she did to Him? That's the key: He is saying you don't have to cry anymore, you don't have to weep anymore, you don't have to struggle anymore, you don't have to apologize anymore. Be still and know that He is God.

When I was a little boy, my momma told me, "Son, don't make it hard for folks to say 'I'm sorry.'" Don't make it hard for someone

to apologize to you when they've done you wrong. You're every bit
as human as they are. You mess up, too. You need complete forgiveness, too. I was once going out with this girl and she really
hurt me, cut my heart deep. She called one day and my momma
told me she was on the phone.

"I don't want to talk to her," I said.

Then she called another day and invited me to a party.

I told my momma, "I'm not going to any party where she is."

And momma responded, "Son, that's her way of saying 'I'm
sorry.' Don't make it hard for her to say she's sorry."

God sings you a love song and He never makes it hard for you
to say, "Father, I'm sorry." What an amazing love. Use your sanctified imagination for a moment and visualize God singing over
you. He receives you and forgives you and rejoices over your return; and then He sings over you, sings to you, and sings for you.

If you are younger and don't have a lot of experience with love,
then I can promise you that when you do gain more experience,
you will find that there will be problems, it will get ragged, it will
get difficult, it will get very trying. The problem is that you
thought it was always going to be kissy-kissy, and you never imagined it was going to turn *really bad*. But somewhere down the line,
every relationship goes from kissy-kissy to "Kiss my [blank]!" At
some point in that relationship, because we are human, the love af-
fair gets messed up and somebody has got to be big enough to
take the high road and love you like Jesus does—unconditionally,
without retribution, with full forgiveness. Because when *you* mess
up, He loves you anyway. And when you come back, He forgives
you and He loves you like He didn't even know what you did. But
you know what you did, and He knows what you did; Yet He acts
like nothing ever happened, because He loves you so much.

It is crucial that you understand that God's love for you is so
strong that He embraces you, looks you in the eyes, and says, "Welcome home, baby. Welcome home." He sings a love song over you.

The prophet Zephaniah says God will cover you and love you
and rejoice over you with singing. I want that kind of lover—I want
to *be* that kind of lover, where the spirit of my love gets tough with

a heart of compassion and forgiveness and refuses to give up. I want to be a lover who can admit, "Yes, you hurt me. But I love you with a love that is everlasting." That's tough love.

Imagine God covering you with His song, cuddling you with His singing as He sings over you. Sometimes we aren't even aware of it, yet God is serenading us. When I think about how good God has been to me in spite of the times I stepped over the line and went astray and walked in disobedience and turned my back on Him and went after frivolous and ungodly temptations, yet He still covered me with his love . . . that is absolutely amazing to me. Think about that. He reaches out to a lover who has gone astray. It's as though He comes to get her. It doesn't matter how far she's gone from him. There are times when Israel had fallen into the depths of degradation. The Israelites who knew Him were living just like the Gentiles who knew nothing about God. They were just as low as the heathen. Yet God has a love that could reach so low that He would reach down into our pit and love us—and then actually sing to us. *Amazing!*

> *You sing all around*
> *But I never hear the sound*
> *Lord, I'm amazed by You*
> *Lord, I'm amazed by You*
> *Lord, I'm amazed by You*
> *How You love me*[1]

God calls you with His everlasting love and delights you with His songs. He comforts you and surrounds you with His love. Picture yourself experiencing and responding to His love as God sings to you. Now *that* is one passionate God.

## REFLECTION QUESTIONS

1. What things might prompt God to sing?

2. Why did God want the Israelites to write down songs for themselves and teach it to their children?

3. How would you define "teach it forward" discipleship?

4. When was a time in your life that your heart sang with love for God?

**Note**
1. Phillips, Craig and Dean, "Amazed" (Columbia, 2006).

Kenneth C. Ulmer

# The God Who Cares

*Maschil of David; a Prayer when he was in the cave. I cried unto the*
*LORD with my voice; with my voice unto the LORD did I make my*
*supplication. I poured out my complaint before him; I showed before him*
*my trouble. When my spirit was overwhelmed within me, then thou*
*knewest my path. In the way wherein I walked have they privily laid a*
*snare for me. I looked on my right hand, and beheld, but there was no*
*man that would know me: refuge failed me; no man cared for my soul.*
*I cried unto thee, O LORD: I said, Thou art my refuge and my portion in*
*the land of the living. Attend unto my cry; for I am brought very low:*
*deliver me from my persecutors; for they are stronger than I.*
*Bring my soul out of prison, that I may praise thy name: the righteous*
*shall compass me about; for thou shalt deal bountifully with me.*
PSALM 142, *KJV*

Can you think of a problem you have that God doesn't know
about? Can you think of a problem you have that God does not
care about? Can you think of a problem you have that God is pow-
erless to do something about? These are three questions you will
wrestle with from time to time, no matter who you are. No matter
your status in life. No matter the extent of your biblical education.
No matter how long or to what degree you have lived a religious
spiritual life. "Does God care?" is a question that will appear time
and time again.

I believe that one of the craftiest strategies the enemy throws
at Christians to weaken our walk with the Lord when we're facing
challenges, struggles and trials in life is to lead us into concluding
that God doesn't care about us. The devil wants to convince you

that what you are going through is beyond God's radar, that you're in this thing by yourself, that God has more important people and situations to deal with and really doesn't care about you. It is about just such an experience that David wrote Psalm 142, as a "plea for relief from persecutors."

Keep in mind that all of the psalms are but songs. But the 142nd psalm is unique in this collection of 150 psalms, because the psalm doesn't begin with verse one. It, like several others, begins with the designation, or category, of this particular song. In most Bibles, under the Psalm 142, you will find the word *maschil*, which means that this psalm is one of a unique group of 13 psalms out of the 150 psalms that are *maschil* psalms. *Maschil* means "an instruction," "a teaching." This song, this psalm, is a didactic poem, a psalm or song composed specifically to teach something.

The next thing you find at the beginning of this *maschil* is that it is a prayer of David. So, first, it is a *maschil*; and second, it is a prayer. Then the designation says that this *maschil* psalm is related to a cave ("when David was in the cave"). This is the only psalm in this final collection of Davidic psalms (see Pss. 138–145) that provides the reader with a setting: "*Maschil* of David; a Prayer when he was in the cave." The setting is helpful for our understanding of the psalm, since we know something about David's situation at this time (see 1 Sam. 22:1-2). Even more, it makes Psalm 142 a companion to Psalm 57, which likewise begins: "Of David. A *miktam*. When he had fled from Saul into the cave." So, we now understand that the message of this psalm does not begin with verse 1, but refers to something that occurred before verse 1. Thus, Psalm 142 begins with the designation and categorization of the song, which is labeled as a *maschil*.

Some truths are subtle, and we almost catch them by accident; but others come forth intentionally. Certainly all of the psalms (and all of Scripture) are good for instruction. But the *maschil* psalms are intentionally created to teach something. David, the composer, has experienced something and he assumes that someone else will go through what he's been through, so he writes this song, these lyrics, in order to pass on what he had learned. The song becomes a vehicle for instruction, an educational tool, a synthesis of song and teaching.

David gives the realities of his situation, which he assumes will be like that of somebody else. He says he's in a cave. Then, in verse 7, he says he's in a prison. He calls this cave a prison. So this song was written in David's cave season, his prison season, when he was fleeing and hiding from the enemy. David, the anointed king and leader of the people of God, the one chosen by the Lord to shepherd the sheep of Israel, is literally living in a cave because the present king, Saul, is a jealous hater.

Saul sees David coming along, yet he knows God has His hand on the young future king, so he doesn't simply want to hurt David, he wants to take him out. Nine times he tried to outright kill David. It was Saul's jealousy that caused David to have to literally run for his life. So here is this great king, great warrior, man of God, King David, who is on the run and living in a cave.

## Alone in the Cave

On two occasions, David hid out in caves. One was a cave near a place called the Valley of the Shadow, where the nearby hills and mountains are interspersed with many caves. The second time David hid in a cave was a desert area called En-gedi, near the Crags of the Wild Goats, where the surrounding hills are filled with caves. It was in one of those caves, called Adullam (see 1 Sam. 22:1), where David wrote Psalm 142, as a symbolic teaching tool for anyone else who would come to a cave. Spiritually, it speaks of those of us who, at one time or another, go through "cave seasons" when we feel imprisoned.

Even in the presence of the Lord and in the midst of worshiping and praising God's name, you might be in a metaphorical cave, imprisoned by something that exerts a control from which you cannot escape. Maybe you are imprisoned by your passions and can't control your cravings—drugs, alcohol, sex, money, power. You're a prisoner as surely as if you were in handcuffs. Maybe you've tried, time and time again to shake it, but you remain locked up as though you were imprisoned in a jail cell. Or maybe you're imprisoned in your position, and it feels like your life is struck. You can't get out, can't move forward. You're on hold. You're in a prison of circumstance.

In this psalm, David says, "I've been there, I've done that, and let me share with you what I've learned." Symbolically, he says that he is surrounded by enemies. They keep on coming because Saul won't give up. He keeps pursuing and pursuing and he never gets tired. So David is always on the run, constantly surrounded by a mounting number of enemies. But more than that, he is standing alone.

In verse 4, he sings, "I looked on my right" (*KJV*). That's important because the position on the right is the position of a defender. In courtroom scenes, the defense attorney, the advocate of the accused, sits on the right side of the defendant. David says he looked to his right side and nobody was there. He pictures himself in a cave, on the run from the enemy, standing alone. Times are bad. But to go through bad times by yourself makes bad times even worse.

Have you ever been through something that was so messed up that you couldn't even understand it? You would have called somebody if you knew somebody who would understand what you were going through. People told you, "Well . . . just trust Jesus. You're going to be all right." *No, I'm not going to be alright—you're not going through what I'm going through!* Or there have been times when you couldn't even think of somebody to call. David looked around and there was no one standing with him. Here's the catch: David was not literally alone, but it is implied within the historical context of this psalm (not in the actual verse) that in the cave with him were 400 of his followers (see 1 Sam. 22:2). David was hiding out on the run, but he was not literally all alone, because he had a few warriors with him interspersed throughout the maze of caves. These are soldiers who move when he says "Move!" and go when he says "Go!" and fight when he says "Fight!" Yet, he said, "I'm alone."

Have you ever been in a crowd, yet you felt like you were on an island all by yourself? It's not that you didn't see the people there—

you saw them all over the place. But you didn't see anyone who knew what you were going through. David was the anointed king, yet he was forced to hide out like a convict. Have you ever gone through something that you felt nobody could relate to? And even if you told them, no one would understand—not really.

Physically, David was in a situation where he felt as if he were all by himself. Emotionally, he said his spirit was overwhelmed. "I am brought very low," He wrote (v. 6, *KJV*). He's crying out because he's in trouble. It's a multifaceted picture of depression. His spirit is overwhelmed. The word means "to be faint," "to be feeble," "to cave in." Circumstances are falling in on him. He's trapped, and nobody can relate to what he's going through. There are 400 men around him, but not one of them really recognizes who he is. Look at how various Bible translations describe David's mindset in verse 4:

- *TLB*: "No one gives me a passing thought. No one will help me; no one cares a bit what happens to me."
- *NRSV*: "There is no one who takes notice of me; no refuge remains to me; no one cares for me."
- *NIV*: "No one is concerned for me. I have no refuge; no one cares for my life."
- *NCV*: "No one cares about me. I have no place of safety; no one cares if I live."
- *NASB*: "For there is no one who regards me; there is no escape for me; no one cares for my soul."
- *NKJV*: "There is no one who acknowledges me; refuge has failed me; no one cares for my soul."

The places and the people I went to, he says, have failed me. I've tried everything else and I've come to the conclusion that nobody even cares for my soul. The term *cares for* means "to go after," "to seek for." It reflects an effort to find; it means being concerned enough to take action to find me. David has been on the lam for months, hiding out here and there, running everywhere. And He's the king—God had anointed him! Yet here's what David says: *No one even cares if I live!* No one has even come looking for me. No one

put out a search committee. The man is a king! How long could
you go missing without anybody missing you?

## Soul Business

It's interesting how David kicks it up a notch by saying, "No one
cares for my soul." He's lamenting not just that nobody seems to
care where he is or whether he's alive or dead, destroyed or flour-
ishing; he says, "Nobody cares for my *soul*." That's a depth of despair that goes beyond thinking, *Poor me, nobody cares.* This goes
to his core, to his very being, the breath of life given to him by
God Himself.

Jesus said, "What will it profit a man if he gains the whole
world, and loses his own soul?" (Mark 8:36). Whose soul are you
concerned about? Discipleship is soul business. It doesn't matter
how cute and fine a person is; what about his or her soul? We read
in Ezekiel 18:20, "The soul who sins shall die." That means that
someone will die and go to hell. Many of us know people who will
go to hell, and some of us don't give a damn. (And some people
reading these words are more upset at that second statement than
at the first one.) There are people in the lives of many of us who
will die and go to hell because we don't care enough about their
souls to even attempt to do anything about it. Some people are
even married to a spouse whose insurance policy they care more
about than their spouse's soul. That's a sad comment on the level
of caring in today's generation, but it's true.

I love King David. He often spoke out of both sides of his
scriptural mouth: "Look on my right hand and see, for there is no
one who acknowledges me" (Ps. 142:4). Then he says, "I cried out
to You, O LORD: I said, 'You are my refuge, My portion in the land
of the living'" (v. 5). *I looked, God. Now You look. And when You look,
God, you'll see there's no one.* Have you ever been through something
and you wondered if God missed it? David is saying, *I can see that
nobody is standing with me.* Then he cries out to God, saying, "Hey,
You see this?" (Remember, this is a prayer. Don't take it out of context.) "Do you see that nobody's standing with me, Lord?" Some-

times you have a prayer life where you haven't got time to say all that fancy stuff and properly articulate what's going on. Sometimes you blurt out, *What's up!?* Now, David is a little schizophrenic, because he'll tell you one thing and then turn around and say something else. Because then he says to God, in verse three, "You knew my path."

As I noted before, one of the problems about Scripture is you can't always tell the emotions underpinning the text. What you get here is that David comes up against God, tells Him nobody is there, nobody cares, everyone has failed him . . . and then he remembers Who he's talking to and he says, in verse five, "You are my refuge, My portion in the land of the living." In modern vernacular, this could be read, "Do You see what's going on, God? But I know You got my back, because you know my path." The phrase "You know my path" means this: God knows the path where David treads, He knows this road, He has traveled this road Himself. In spite of all that's going on, David knows one thing: The Lord knows his way.

In verse 3, David says, "They have secretly set a snare for me." *There are traps on this road, and You, God, know where the traps are!* David is calling on God for guidance. Lead me around the trips and traps and tricks. Sometimes we need to acknowledge that we don't know where we're going. That's when we call out, Lord, help me make it through this mess!

But there's another spin to "You know my way": You know how I am. David is saying to God, *You know where my limit is, and I've got just one raw nerve left—and this situation is about to get on it!* God knows David's breaking point. "I'm not sure if You're here, God, but I know You know me. I know You wouldn't let me face something I can't handle on my own. If I couldn't handle this, You wouldn't place this on me. You know I'm afraid. You know I'm weak and need You right now, Lord."

There may have been times in your life when you went to God and said, "Wait a minute! I don't know how much more I can take of this, God." And you come back a week later, saying, "I can't take anymore of this!" Then a month later, six months later, you say, "I can't take it anymore." And then you realize that you have "taken it" longer that you thought you could. And a year later, all is well. You realize that with God, you can not only take it—you can make it! God will not allow you to face anything that you cannot handle as long you know He cares and has His hand on you.

"Lord, You know me" means three things: (1) God knows your journey, (2) God knows how you are, and (3) God knows the road you're on.

And if He knows the road that got you in it, He knows the road that will get you out of it. "Yea, though I walk through the valley of the shadow of death . . ." (Ps. 23:4).

By the end, in verse seven, David is saying, *Bring my soul out. Set me free! Get me out of here!* Why is he saying this? Why do you want to get delivered? Why do you want to get out of your mess? Why do you want to come through the problems you are facing? Why do you want God to lift that load from your weary shoulders and pull you through? David makes that answer crystal clear at the end of the *maschil*: So that he "may praise Your name" (v. 7).

## Cast Your Cares on God

Each of us, at some time or another, will find ourselves in cave and prison seasons. Does God care about that? The lesson of Psalm 142, through the teaching given us through King David, is a resounding *yes*—God is the God who cares. He knows your way, He knows your journey, and He knows how you are. Your response to such a God who cares so much should be, as Apostle Peter stated it so succinctly in 1 Peter 5:7, to cast "the whole of your care [all your anxieties, all your worries, all your concerns, once and for all] on Him, for He cares for you" (1 Pet. 5:7, *AMP*). The word "cast" means "to toss" or "to throw." It's the picture that is used in the New Testament of when Jesus came to Jerusalem riding on a donkey. They threw articles of clothing up on the back of the colt. They made a saddle for Jesus. They threw something on the animal He could sit on so He could control it. Cast your cares onto Him, for He cares for you.

David is teaching you, from his experience, that when you throw your stuff onto God, when you toss your burden on Him, when you give over to Him your troubles, your agony, all those things that keep you up all night, He will lead you through. Because He cares for you. David paints the picture of a man who is depressed and despondent and struggling with emotional pain. But he hears the word of the Lord saying, *Cast your stuff onto Me and I will sustain you, I will hold you, I will carry you through.*

You might be familiar with the allegorical text referred to as "Footprints in the Sand," where a man sees, during the journey of his life, two sets of footprints, side by side, one set of which disappears. The man concludes that the disappearing footprints were during the worst time of his life—and that was when Jesus had abandoned him. *Why would Jesus leave me?* the man wonders. The Lord answers, *When there was only one set of footprints in the sand, I picked you up and carried you through your troubles.*

David tells God to get him out of there and take him to a place where he can praise Him. Take him away from the pain and into the praise. David knows what follows praise: "For You shall deal bountifully with me" (Ps. 142:7). Thus, he closes out the lesson of this psalm: God will surround you with the righteous, He will sustain you by putting around you people who love you enough to see you come out of the cave. And when you come out, they will start rejoicing just like they just got released themselves. We need folks in our life who know how to celebrate with us. You need some people who won't envy you when God is ready to bless you. David said He looked around and the enemy was rising, but God was right there with him.

I don't care what you're going through in your life, my friend, *God cares.* I don't know how dark it is in your situation, how confusing it is, He cares for you, because He is a caring God. And because He cares, you can cast your cares on Him and he will handle your stuff. But the key is that you've got to throw Him something. You've got to realize that you need to trust God with your burdens. Even people with a few college degrees and several initials behind their name are out of work these days. In God there is refuge. If you've tried everything else, try God. Toss Him your job, your skills, your talents. He'll take you from a place of pain to a place of praise. God cares, no matter how tight of a situation you are in.

Not long ago, my son and I were in Dallas, where we met a man who had been in jail for 34 years of a life sentence he had received for killing a woman. But the man was innocent. His defense attorney, a public defender, had advised him to agree to the District Attorney's plea bargain offer instead of going through the uncertainty and turmoil of a trial. The man refused to accept the plea, insisting that he was innocent. But the jury found him guilty and gave him life in prison. In an unheard of move many years after the death of the judge who had originally sentenced the man, the judge who had heard the final appeal reviewed the case. The judge ruled that the man had been innocent all along and ordered him released.

When I met the man, I asked him, "How in the world did you make it through thirty four years behind bars, knowing that you were innocent?"

"Well," he replied, "the rest of the story is that I got saved in prison. I got filled with the Holy Spirit there and started a Bible study." He hadn't been saved but a few months when he began the study group and started to disciple other prisoners—more than a thousand men during his decades of being wrongfully incarcerated. And then God released him.

I heard the tape of when he called his spiritual father after he was released. He was crying like a baby. "Dad," he wept, "I'm out." Surrounding him was a group of other people who had come to the court. He was praising God on the phone, and in the background you could hear other people praising God with him for his deliverance. They had never been to jail themselves, but they were celebrating the fact that he had been released from prison with the faithful help of so many people.

What is it in your life that you will acknowledge you can't handle all by yourself? This is not pride time. This is for those who realize they are trapped in something they can't control and can't get out of it by themselves. It could be a drug habit, an alcohol habit, a sex habit, a power habit, a money habit or just being chased by a devil. David said to cast your cares on God as the enemy mounts up to make a run at you. God will lift up your head (see Ps. 3:3). God is the one who will step into your situation and lead you to a place of praise where He gets all the glory for caring enough about you to deliver you.

Nine times Saul tried to kill David, and failed. David could have killed Saul a few times too, but he refused—even when he had gotten close enough in that cave called Adullam and stealthily cut off the corner of Saul's royal robe just to show Saul that he could have killed him. Instead, David bows his head, leaves the vengeance up to God, his countenance low, and looks up to the Lord, declaring like a psalmist, "Attend to my cry, for I am brought very low; deliver me from my persecutors, for they are stronger than I. Bring my soul out of prison, that I may praise Your name; the righteous shall surround me, for You shall deal bountifully with me." And so God did.

> *Cast your burden on the LORD, and He shall sustain you;*
> *He shall never permit the righteous to be moved.*
> PSALM 55:22

# REFLECTION QUESTIONS

1. What is a *maschil*?

2. What does it mean that God knows you?

3. When was a time in your life when you thought God didn't care?

4. What was the outcome of that situation?

# CONCLUSION

# God Is Passionate . . .
# That's Why We Are

The love of God is simply the most amazing, exciting reality in the universe. I am often overwhelmed by His love. Sometimes, during an early morning walk, or in my late-night chill time, or even at 36,000 feet in the air on a ministry assignment somewhere in God's world, I have almost laughed at myself to the point where tears well up in my eyes at the mere thought of how much God loves me. There is a saying, one of those churchy clichés in the African American tradition, that goes like this: "When I think about the goodness of Jesus, and all He has done for me, my soul cries out." If you ever get a glimpse, just the briefest idea, of the greatness of the love of God, I promise you, it will change your life. It will humble you, inspire you, encourage you and bless you.

Romans 8:29 explains that a life committed to God is a process of becoming more and more like Jesus. Growing in the image and likeness of Christ, becoming more like Him, includes learning to love like God loves us. As we love more like Him, we grow; and as we grow, we love more like Him. We learn to love by learning and imitating the love with which God loves us.

One of the first songs I learned as a little boy going to Sunday School at Mt. Zion Baptist Church in East St. Louis, Illinois, was a song that taught me something about love. We began this literary journey by recollecting one of the world's greatest artists of the time, Ms. Whitney Houston. One of the last songs Whitney sang was that same song that I learned as a boy in Sunday School. There are 13 psalms in the Bible identified as a "maschil," a song psalm composed for the specific purpose of teaching a lesson. Although

it is not officially labeled a *maschil*, the little song I learned, the
song Whitney sang, the song you may know, is a simple little
maschil that goes like this:

> *Jesus loves me! This I know, for the Bible tells me so.*
> *Little ones to Him belong; they are weak, but He is strong.*
> *Yes, Jesus loves me!*
> *Yes Jesus loves me!*
> *Yes Jesus loves me!*
> *The Bible tells me so.*[1]

Another Sunday School song we learned (which seemed to be
a musical response to "Jesus Loves Me") functioned as another
*maschil* for me:

> *O how I love Jesus,*
> *O how I love Jesus,*
> *O how I love Jesus,*
> *Because He first loved me!*[2]

I used to think this song meant that I respond to God's love
and I love Him, because before I loved him, He loved me. But I don't
believe that's the gist of the teaching about God's love. As I have
grown in the Lord, I have begun to realize that there is a slightly
different spin on the interpretation of this classic hymn. When the
Bible says, "We love Him because He first loved us," (1 John 4:19),
I believe it speaks of the ability that God gives us, the model He
gives us, through Jesus. It's not that we love in some mechanical,
automatic response to His love. Rather, it is that our relationship
with the Lord (which John also depicts as a relationship of Divine
indwelling) becomes the empowerment and example of love.

As 1 John 4:4 states, "You are of God, little children . . . because
He who is in you is greater than he who is in the world." He who
is in us is He who is love (see 1 John 4:7). It is the love in us that
loves others through us. So, rather than my love being the response to the love of Christ, the "Christ in me" (see Col. 1:27) is al-

ready my example and model of love. Therefore, I learn to love because He who *is* love and is *in* me teaches me how to love. And, as I am being progressively conformed and shaped into the image of my Lord, I ask Him to teach me how to love like Him.

All of mankind is made in the image of God the Creator—although that perfect image was marred by sin (though there is still His "DNA Godness" in each of us). So, since God loves with a love that is prone to jealousy and anger, maybe that's why we often love with a jealous love—albeit a love that is rooted in the frailty of human fallenness and tainted with sin and the effects thereof.

As we have examined in these pages, the love of God is multidimensional. Yet the many dimensions of godly love are always in the balance of His perfect character. That's why He knows, for example, suffering and grief, and He also rejoices and laughs. Our goal, then, must be to make His kind of love our kind of love; to love like Him, unfettered in all of its dimensions and expressions—yet always underpinned with His unconditionally giving heart. In other words, we need to learn to get angry only at what makes Him angry; to be able to sing while we rest in Him; to be able to rejoice from motivations like His; to laugh for reasons He would laugh.

In this book, I have tried to plumb the depths of the unfathomable love of God for us. I want to wrap up this trip on the Bible Bus (a term I borrow from the late Dr. J. Vernon McGee) by brief reexamination of Philippians 3:10, wherein Apostle Paul declares his heart's desire to walk closer to the Lord and to have his life reflect the life of Christ on a more intimate and profound level: "That I may know Him and the power of His resurrection, and the fellowship of His sufferings, being conformed to His death." Paul expands on the idea of resurrection power in his letter to the first-century Ephesians. He stacks word on word as he enthusiastically describes the power available to believers through the Holy Spirit. He wants the readers to know and understand and receive "the exceeding greatness of his *power* toward us who believe, according to the *working* of His *mighty power*" (Eph. 1:19, emphasis added). I have italicized the words power, working and mighty power—all different words (in the Greek, *dúnamis, enérgeia, krátos, ischús*), yet all synonyms for one word: *power*. Paul wants you to know the resurrection power that is available to you right now. It is the same power that resurrected Jesus Christ from the dead—and I guarantee you that any problem, trial, struggle or challenge you are facing is far less than a dead Jesus. But if God could handle a dead Jesus, then you and He together can certainly handle *all* of your problems.

*Passion is power is God.* You serve a powerful God who does not hesitate to display His passion concerning you, for you are His beloved creation.

> *We may affirm absolutely that nothing great in the world has been accomplished without passion.*
> GEORG WILHELM FRIEDRICH HEGEL (1770-1831)

**Notes**
1. Anna Bartlett Warner, "Jesus Loves Me," (1860), cited in William B. Bradbury, *The New National Baptist Hymnal* (Nashville, TN: National Baptist Publishing Board, 1977), p. 465.
2. Frederick Whitfield, "O How I Love Jesus" (1855), cited in Bradbury, *The New National Baptist Hymnal,* p. 10.

# About the Author

For more than 30 years, Kenneth C. Ulmer, Ph.D., has been Senior Pastor of Faithful Central Bible Church in Los Angeles. He is also past President of The King's University in Los Angeles (where he is a founding board member, Vice Chairman of the Board, Adjunct Professor of Preaching and Leadership, and serves as Dean of The King's Oxford University Summer Program, England). In 2000, Dr. Ulmer's church acquired The Great Western Forum (previous home of the Lakers professional basketball team), which the ministry operated as a commercial entertainment venue for more than a decade.

Dr. Ulmer participated in the study of Ecumenical Liturgy and Worship at Magdalene College at Oxford University, has served as an instructor in Pastoral Ministry and Homiletics at Grace Theological Seminary, as an instructor of African-American Preaching at Fuller Theological Seminary, as an adjunct professor at Biola University (where he served on the Board of Trustees), and as an adjunct professor at Pepperdine University. He also served as a mentor in the Doctor of Ministry Degree Program at United Theological Seminary, in Ohio.

He received his Bachelor of Arts degree in Broadcasting and Music from the University of Illinois. After accepting his call to the ministry, Dr. Ulmer was ordained at Mount Moriah Missionary Baptist Church in Los Angeles, and shortly afterward founded Macedonia Bible Baptist Church in San Pedro, California. He has studied at Pepperdine University, Hebrew Union College, the University of Judaism and Christ Church, and Magdalene College at Oxford University. He earned a Ph.D. from Grace Graduate School of Theology, in Long Beach, California (west coast campus of Grace Theological Seminary), and his Doctor of Ministry from United Theological Seminary. He was awarded an Honorary Doctor of Divinity degree from Southern California School of Ministry.

Pastor Ulmer was consecrated as Bishop of Christian Education of the Full Gospel Baptist Church Fellowship, where he served on the Bishops' Council. He has served on the Board of Directors of The Gospel Music Workshop of America, the Pastor's Advisory Council to the mayor of the City of Inglewood, California, and on the Board of Trustees of Southern California School of Ministry. In 2012, he participated in Dialogue on Global Ecumenism in Rome, and he currently serves as Presiding Bishop over Macedonia International Bible Fellowship, based in Johannesburg, South Africa, which is an association of pastors representing ministries in South Africa, Jerusalem, and the U.S.

Dr. Ulmer is the associate editor of *The New Spirit Filled Life Bible* (Thomas Nelson), and has written several books, including: *Knowing God's Voice: Learn How to Hear God Above the Chaos of Life and Respond Passionately in Faith; Making Your Money Count: Why We Have It & How to Manage It* (wise financial management for today's Christians); *A New Thing* (a reflection on the Full Gospel Baptist movement); *Spiritually Fit to Run the Race* (a guide to godly living); *In His Image: An Intimate Reflection of God* (an update of his book, *The Anatomy of God*); *The Champion in You* (developing champions for God's Kingdom on Earth); and *The Power of Money: How to Avoid a Devil's Snare*. He is also a recipient of The King's College Apostelos Christou Award, which is presented annually to leaders who characterize the passion and values of the Christian faith through leadership that has notably penetrated the contemporary culture.

Dr. Ulmer is served in all literary endeavors by writer M. Rutledge McCall (see http://www.MRutledgeMcCall.com).

# God Is Speaking...
# Will You Listen?

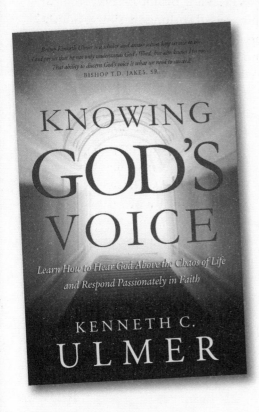

**Knowing God's Voice**
Kenneth C. Ulmer, Ph.D.
ISBN 978-0-8307-5890-6
ISBN 0-8307-5890-9

We know that healthy give-and-take relationships do not happen when one person does all the talking. So why do so many Christians forget to let God get a word in edgewise? If you're like many believers, you may not know how to listen for and respond in faith to the voice of God. But now, in *Knowing God's Voice*, Dr. Kenneth C. Ulmer shows you how to hear from God and act on His words. It may be difficult sometimes, in the midst of all that you are facing, to feel confident that the Almighty takes a personal interest in your life. *Knowing God's Voice* provides the assurance you have been waiting for: God is interested, and He has a lot to say in return! In these pages, you will learn to discern God's voice from the background noise of internal anxiety and external circumstances, and to trust His guidance and revelation even in trying times. God is speaking to His people, if only we will have ears to hear!

# What Is True Biblical Prosperity?

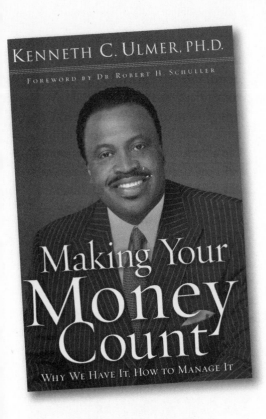

**Making Your Money Count:**
**Why We Have It, How to Manage It**
Kenneth C. Ulmer, Ph.D.
ISBN 978-0-8307-4376-6
ISBN 0-8307-4376-6

In the area of finances, our decision to go it alone by not following God's ways is what relegates many of us to struggle to live paycheck to paycheck as have-nots. But in Scripture, God gives us full guidance and instructions, processes and commands on how to live our life and deal with just about every conceivable situation that we might encounter. However, He never forces us to follow His ways—even though experience shows that His ways are always best for our ultimate peace, happiness, productivity and success. In this groundbreaking look at the parables of the talents and the man of noble birth, pastor, teacher and author Dr. Kenneth Ulmer reveals Christ's call to us to "do business" for Him. Follow Dr. Ulmer's biblical prescription to see the many blessings that await those who faithfully take care of business and make their money count.